Double Cream

By

Robert Taylor & Joyce Worsfold

Joyce Worsfold and Robert Taylor are brother and sister and have spent most of their working lives teaching children in Yorkshire. They have written together since child-hood, producing poetry, stories, plays, musicals, song lyrics and monologues.
Over 30 years they have performed their work for many audiences mostly in the North of England and Scotland, delighting thousands and bringing them both laughter and tears.

This book is full of what it is all about. The *Cream,* of the poetry, stories and monologues Robert and Joyce have produced over the years for adults – hence the title of the book – *Double Cream.'*

Their many previously published books include –

Not another ball pool
Shark attack (the poems are back!)
Donkeys, ducks and daily bread
The Goolagong Gang Stories
Interludes

'Double Cream' is written by Robert Taylor & Joyce Worsfold © 2011. Cover photograph by Lauren Parry.

Published by Dangeroo Publishing.
Printed by Jedburgh Press.
ISBN : 9780955926044

£4.99

~ Contents ~

Poem	Author	Page
Then	Joyce Worsfold	7
A woman for all time	Robert Taylor & Mike Hone	8
The Christmas gift	Joyce Worsfold	9
Valentines	Joyce Worsfold	10
Love is opening new windows	Robert Taylor	11
Interludes	Robert Taylor & Mike Hone	12
The Natural Curriculum	Joyce Worsfold	13
Sonnet	Joyce Worsfold	16
Birth	Robert Taylor	17
Not very P.C.	Joyce Worsfold	18
Winking!	Robert Taylor	19
Learning light	Joyce Worsfold	20
In the mirror	Robert Taylor	21
The games of life	Joyce Worsfold	22
I used to say that!	Robert Taylor	23
Saturday Matinee	Joyce Worsfold	24
Fireworks night	Robert Taylor	26
Strange incident at 460	Robert Taylor	27
Old masters	Joyce Worsfold	28
The boxing glove	Joyce Worsfold	29
Dad's singing	Robert Taylor	30
A mum with less brains	Robert Taylor	31
A tale of a toilet	Joyce Worsfold	32
Boy scout camp	Joyce Worsfold	33
Cayton Bay	Robert Taylor	34
When I grow up	Joyce Worsfold	37
A cat in school	Robert Taylor	39
Playground Duty	Joyce Worsfold	40
A Colossal thing	Robert Taylor	41
Can we write us news?	Joyce Worsfold	43
Children like me	Robert Taylor	45
Bones!	Robert Taylor	46
Saturated	Joyce Worsfold	47
School theatre visit	Joyce Worsfold	48
Chinese Whispers	Joyce Worsfold	50
Towards plain English	Robert Taylor	51
A choice of careers	Robert Taylor	52
Being shown the ropes	Robert Taylor	53
The cat with two p's	Robert Taylor	55
Robert's train	Joyce Worsfold	56
Compost	Joyce Worsfold	57
Timothy's arm	Joyce Worsfold	58
ABC Poem	Joyce Worsfold	59

Oh for a quiet life	Robert Taylor	60
Can anybody here do this sum?	Robert Taylor	61
Mice	Joyce Worsfold	63
Quatrain	Joyce Worsfold	65
The Caretaker (story)	Robert Taylor	66
Unfinished symphony	Joyce Worsfold	68
Oh dear! What can the matter be?	Robert Taylor	70
Embroidery	Joyce Worsfold	71
A blind God	Joyce Worsfold	71
A multicultural education	Joyce Worsfold	72
No feelings	Robert Taylor	75
A funny name for God	Robert Taylor	76
Thunder cloud	Joyce Worsfold	78
The Outing	Joyce Worsfold	79
Cold comfort	Joyce Worsfold	80
What goes on in a dog's head	Robert Taylor	83
Fish and chips	Robert Taylor	84
Growing Up	Robert Taylor	86
Ice cream parlour	Joyce Worsfold	87
Ice cold in a coffee shop	Joyce Worsfold	88
That's all we need!	Robert Taylor	89
The Whitby Triangle	Robert Taylor	93
When Arthur came to our school	Robert Taylor	94
Body beautiful	Joyce Worsfold	95
Concentration	Joyce Worsfold	96
A mother's anguished blues	Robert Taylor	97
The road to Mother Care	Joyce Worsfold	98
Children of Africa	Joyce Worsfold	99
Tanks for tea	Joyce Worsfold	100
Barney and Sam	Joyce Worsfold	101
Oldies	Joyce Worsfold	101
Please do it yourself	Robert Taylor	102
That's Life	Robert Taylor	105
A leak in the head	Robert Taylor	107
Bath time	Robert Taylor	107
It didn't work for me	Robert Taylor	108
Burns night	Robert Taylor	110
The Dog walker's lament	Robert Taylor	111
A great Poemer!	Robert Taylor	112
A special day out	Joyce Worsfold	113
George – A Melodrama	Robert Taylor	114
Silent night	Joyce Worsfold	116
Funeral teas	Joyce Worsfold	117
A widow's tale (story)	Robert Taylor	118
My Mum	Robert Taylor	121
All things daffodils	Joyce Worsfold	122
Remembering Rock and Roll	Joyce Worsfold	124
Down the line	Robert Taylor	125

The Photograph (story)	Robert Taylor	126
Breakdown	Joyce Worsfold	128
Going out	Joyce Worsfold	129
Our Joannie	Robert Taylor	131
Michael	Robert Taylor	132
Finale	Joyce Worsfold	133
Death in the high Street	Robert Taylor	134
Afterwards	Joyce Worsfold	135
We are but dust	Robert Taylor & Mike Hone	136

There are 100 poems, monologues and stories here.

*50 by Robert Taylor (3 were song lyrics written with Mike Hone).
50 by Joyce Worsfold.*

Published by Dangeroo Publishing © 2011

Printed by Jedburgh Press
www.jedpress.co.uk

Joyce can be contacted for bookings at
www. joyceworsfoldwrites.com
telephone 01924 840 847

Robert can be contacted for bookings at
www.dangeroo.co.uk
telephone 01830 520 344

Then

Then, you will do it, on that elusive 'one day'
Then, you will finally learn how to play
Then, you will make those pots from clay
Then, you will travel to Bali and Bombay.
Now, is just 'getting ready time'.
Then, you will travel the world and see all it's glories
Then, you will read and paint and run
Then, you will have time for writing stories
Then, you'll drink wine and relax in the sun.

Then, you will do it, when you're retired
Then, you'll be calm and relaxed, not tired
Then, you won't stick in the mud and be mired
Then, your imagination will be free and be fired
Now is a working, working, working time.
Then, you'll spend hours just pottering about the place
Then, you'll have time to take things at a slower pace.
Then, you won't have to hurry and rush and race
Then, you can lie in late without disgrace!

Then, you'll cram in every joy that can be
Then, you will spend time with friends and family
Then, you will listen and share times of quality
Then, life will be fine, just as you want it to be.
Now you are too busy for all that!

BUT...
Then, you might not be physically able
Then, some loved ones will have left the table
Then, you might live in some kind of Babel
Then, might just be a fairytale fable.

Now, is the time to grasp with all your might
Now, today we can plan it all right
Now, is the party, now time to write,
Now time to savour each wonderful bite.
You can fill every precious minute
Yours is the world and everything in it
So take courage, have faith now and 'go for it'
So make love your reason, embrace all that you love
I'm just here to 'give you a shove'.

Joyce Worsfold

A woman for all time

I arrived in Eden and talked with a snake.
I offered Adam an apple was that my mistake?
I moved in to Egypt, where I ruled the Nile.
Threw an empire into confusion,
Then I met another reptile.
I came across an angel on a visit to Earth,
Who said; 'You will be blessed by a virgin birth.'

I'm an all time woman -
a woman for all time.
Perhaps you might just know me?
And be a friend of mine?

I rode against the Roman Empire, in the days of old,
stirring up the British, on my chariot bold.
Then I led my people, while still in my teens.
I was burnt at the stake and they made a saint out of me.
I was the last of six wives, so what new good I give?
I lived in great fear, but my husband I outlived.

I'm an all time woman -
a woman for all time.
Perhaps you might just know me?
And be a friend of mine?

At the turn of the last century, it was crazy you know.
I could bear him fifteen children but I still could not vote.
I've been a slave through the centuries,
Second class and abused.
As the longest serving monarch, I was certainly not amused.
I was the lady of the lamp, dedicated to a cause.
I was amongst the weeping millions, made widows by world wars.

I'm an all time woman-
a woman for all time.
Perhaps you might just know me?
And be a friend of mine?

Robert Taylor with Mike Hone

The Christmas Gift

What would I like for Christmas?
Well! a sweater would be rather nice
There's some nice ones in Marks
and well worth the price
Or a nice warm scarf or a pair of gloves
or records or a real good book, or.........
Sorry, what did you say?
You'd thought about a saviour
You're giving one away!
Well, I don't know
do I really need one?
Will it fit into my life?
I haven't got a lot of space
or a lot of time
Still if it's wrapped up nice
it'll be a welcome surprise
After all, it's the thought that counts
not the prize.
What? there'll be no wrapping paper
it will be in the raw
cold in the stable
wind blowing through the door,
Oh, well, if you say so
But even the smallest things are more acceptable
if prettily wrapped
and you said it would be a tiny thing
and shiny paper, bright ribbons
would make it fit for a king..........
What do you mean, tiny at first?
You mean it will grow!
Listen, I don't want anything that will disrupt
or make a noise
I don't want anything that will interfere with my freedom of choice
My life is organised and tidy
there's a joint on Sunday and bingo on Friday
Will this Saviour fit in with all that?
Christmas is a time of enjoyment ·
not for being knocked flat
No violence or prejudice, everything in it's place
Colour? Well it would be white of course
with a gently smiling face.
Anyway, what's it's purpose?
Will it be of use?
Will it give happiness, ward off abuse?
Will it be a lucky charm?

Will it shelter me from harm?
What? it might bring me trouble
suffering and pain
It might make me look at everything again.
Look, leave me the presents and the tree
The mince-pies and the cake.
Leave me the carols and the children wide awake
Leave me the trappings and the frills,
I'll have to think about the other,
the love that spills
the centre of all things within the candy coat
The essence of all meaning
the beginning of love and hope
I'll have to ask myself............
am I ready for a saviour?

Joyce Worsfold

Valentines

'Valentines' it said, 'buy one get one free'
Well, that's one for him and then one for whom?
Will he buy like this for me?
What on earth would I want with two?
'Look at this' I say to the check-out girl,
'This is encouraging infidelity!'
She says, 'Why not give it a whirl?
They all do it, even royalty!'
I left feeling a bit fragile
But on Valentine's day I wore a smile,
This, 'buy one get one free'
Has provided a bit of a bonanza for me!

Joyce Worsfold

10

Love is opening new windows
(But not closing old doors)

Now we are married, I don't want to stifle you,
Stop you doing your own things,
leave you fat, bored and blue.
There are things we can do together,
but some we must do apart,
We've both got secret desires, we've both got restless hearts.
Sharing should not be all sacrifice,
and it should not be all selfishness.
It should not be two losing, but two into one,
becoming more and not less.

So I'll be a round the world sailor,
and you write a new play.
Tomorrow comes much too soon,
So let us live for each day.
I've got my things to do and I know that you've got yours.
Love is opening new windows, but not closing old doors.

Caring is giving, but having something to give,
And if we can't do that, then we don't know how to live.
Heartaches come someday, it's much better if they're shared,
To halve the load is easier, but you've really got to care.
Crying should not be done alone, but on someone's shoulder,
or in someone's arms.
It should make things warmer, not colder,
It should do good and not harm.

So, you be a round the world sailor,
and I'll write a new play.
Tomorrow comes much too soon,
so let us live for each day.
I've got my things to do and I know that you've got yours.
Love is opening new windows, but not closing old doors.

Robert Taylor

Interludes

From the baby's cry to that old wrinkled face,
There seems a lot of time in between.
But I don't believe it, when I throw away,
On all those ill conceived schemes.

It seems, you've just got to laugh,
and be crazy enough,
to hang on to all of those dreams.

Life is not a one off song.
Home is not a one off place.
Love is not one off interlude,
Between that first cry and that old wrinkled face.

From little toy cars, to slick city bars,
When dolls in the pram, turn to babies,
From war in the park, to war after dark,
A world full of might-be's and maybe's.

You know, you've just got to smile,
and hope in a while,
that things will go the way you want them to.

For life is not a one off song.
Home is not a one off place.
But life can seem like a brief interlude,
Between that first cry and that old wrinkled face.

Robert Taylor with Mike Hone

The Natural Curriculum

The house was amazing and we just stood
Tucked deep in an English bluebell wood.
Excitement mounted as we viewed its vine-clad walls,
The Victorian splendour and elegant halls,
High ceilinged with panelled stairs,
stuffed full of 200 years of prayers.
'Are we really sleeping here tonight?
It's like a palace big and bright.'

We were greeted by our beaming host,
Davina looked as if she'd seen a ghost!
Our new friend explained the rules of the place,
fire regulations, the use of space.
Rooms allocated, the children unpacked
I checked everyone and already was whacked.

Teddy bears and furry cats
all emerged from haversacks.
Disney pyjamas, some even in satin,
big animal slippers and some with a pattern.
Fresh bars of soap and pristine flannels,

'Miss, we've got a tele, but there's only two channels'

'Miss, guess what, we've got a book
in the bedside drawer come and look!'

'It's a Bible Miss, we've all got one
it's all about Jesus, he were God's son.'

'Do we 'ave to read it all tonight,
I'm a slow reader, I'm not very bright!.

Tea was served in an elegant, panelled place
With elaborate cornice, carvings and fire-place
With gold-rimmed china and lots of knives, forks and spoons
and coloured paper napkins, patterned with stars and moons.
There was awe and wonder on every face,
we stood in silence and said grace.

Then excited chatter about starving bellies
as they eyed up gateaux and gibbering jellies.
The chef had pandered to childish taste
and nothing had been prepared in haste.
The sausage well-seasoned and carefully garnished
and twisty chips all quickly vanished.

'Miss, why have we got all these forks and knives?'

'Eh, yer know Henry the eighth, him with all them wives,
did he live here? It feel like he did
and through them panels, that's where they hid'

'I bet there are ghosts, specially in Kevin's room,
Eeh watch it Kev! You'll have to sleep there soon!'

'Bet here's a witch with a spinning wheel,
Or a giant in the attic, there'll be gold to steal.'

So we ate in animated conversation,
Good! Writing session next, no problems with creation.

They wrote with excitement until quite late,
We had atmospheric candles and a fire in the grate.
Then pyjama-clad, with their hair well-brushed,
we curled up by the fire, waiting and hushed.
And we read our stories of myth and magic.
Some were amazing, some funny, some tragic.
We laughed and we cried and listened to what everyone said,
then warmed with hot chocolate went straight off to bed.

Staff positioned on every floor, not much fun,
but it helps curb bouts of knock-a-door and run;
dirty joke telling, hiding other folks shoes,
pillow-fights and homesick blues,
bleeding noses, being sick
Seeing whose got the biggest dick,
apple-pie beds,
bumped heads,
Seeing who can make the rudest noises,
Wailing and howling in venomous voices.

'Miss, miss it isn't fair!
Miss, she's pinched my teddy bear.'

Sir, Simon's made an awful smell
and now Dan's doing it as well!'

'Goodnight, Miss, sleep tight… mind ..the..bugs..don't bite'

A restless night, some ups some downs
nightmares, wet beds, silly clowns,
but as dawn breaks they're raring to go.
It's only half past five and so…
we go for a walk in the bird-brimmed woods,

Identify trees
marvel at bees.
Then stand silent and listen,
Watch the dew on the grass make everything glisten.
Then, through the meadow there leaps a hare.
We hold our breaths, can't believe its there.
Over our heads an owl swoops home,
who knows what creatures around us roam.
A frog hops across our path,
a bullfinch takes a leisurely bath,
puffing up feathers and preening
and all the world is wakened and gleaming.

A hand slides in mine
And an awed voice cries
'Miss, is it always like this, every morning?

'You mean, while you're in your bed grumbling and yawning?
Yes... it's always like this.'

All day we were active, according to our planning,
making wood sculptures, pressing flowers, cramming
each moment with learning and wonder,
delving deep in nature's plunder.
Then there were poems and plays and songs by the fire,
violins and recorders, we were all in the choir.

Then a walk in the dark to look at the stars,
spattered on velvet, *'Look I can see Mars.'*

'No you can't that's the Milky Way
I read about it in the library today.'

'Miss, why are they all named after chocolate bars?'

'Eh! Isn't it quiet I can't hear any cars.'

'How come the sky here is so black
Bet ours isn't when we get back.'

Later we practised being quite still,
so out of the woodland wild-life would spill.
They tried very hard, just an occasional whisper
about pins and needles and the odd little blister.
Bats flew low and a hedgehog shuffled
And a bevy of beasts in the undergrowth rustled.
A fox in the distance stalked its' prey,
we came to the end of a perfect day.

At the end of this precious time together,
we watched from the coach the hills and the heather
and made the most of ant bites and stings,
then snuggled and chatted about our favourite things.
Shameem who is quiet and usually shy
shed tears because we had to say goodbye,
'I used to think Blackpool the best place in the world.
Now I know it's that wood where the squirrel was curled.'

Simon said, *'that fox was cool!'*

Wayne wailed, *'do we have to go back to school?'*

And James whose behaviour usually tries us sore
Said, *'It were the breakfasts, I never had one before.'*

Joyce Worsfold

Sonnet

I awake to green light and know an earthen floor
A rich chorale of birdsong, heralds a new-born day
I shuffle in my sleeping bag, unzip the canvas door.
Dew on grass, rabbits, scent of new-mown hay.
A rattle of billycans and you come into view.
My love, up and dressed, with tender smile,
'Look what I've brought for you.'
You gently lift the lid, I gaze in wonder for a while,
at a perfect tiny being with grey fur, so soft
Ears of finest leather and big bright button eyes
Minute hands so perfect, you hold her up aloft
And seeing all your tenderness, something in me cries.
Some might bring red roses to shout their love out loud
Only you, could bring a field mouse and make me feel so proud.

Joyce Worsfold

Birth

When IT was born there was no room at the stable.
Shepherds stayed in the hills, saw nothing but sheep and grass.
Kings snored tight in their beds;
Counted gold or frolicked with Wednesday wives.
(it was a cloudy night!)

When *IT* was born, God smiled.
(He'd used the mould before!)
There were a few modifications, the odd last revision.
God picked up the old grey matter,
threw in blood, guts and a few other necessities
(like a small brain)
and hacked away.
God sweated profusely.
Wiped his brow and felt pleased when it was over.

When IT was born, there were no hand outs.
No headlines. No historic speeches.
Donkeys sneezed at the first signs.
Women gathered in washing at the first drops;
But no one put out any flags.
IT was only a little birth.
(Though it meant a lot to him!)

'Which way?' *IT* cried, shaking God's right hand. 'Which way?'
And God gave it a compass and pointed to the west.
'How far?' *IT* screamed. 'How far?'
Then God gave it a map, with a scale and a measure.
IT took the map, measured the distance and stared back at God.

God smiled. It seemed a long way.
IT looked at the bellowing, booming mountains,
stared at the steaming, scheming forests.
Heard the lash, crash of waves outside in the black void of the universe;
Where stars screamed , sucked in the light
and moons lay half eaten by darkness.

IT looked back at God and pointed downwards.
'With these?' *IT* asked, pointing at the flimsy,
gossamer wings that God had given him.
'With these?' *IT* repeated, pulling at God's sleeve.
'With those!' said God quietly.
'Nothing is too frail, with *my force* behind it!'

Robert Taylor

17

Not very P.C.

A buttery-gold day
Doorstep hot as new baked bread
Children play in nurses' outfits
Bearing big red crosses
Dolls, gollywogs and bears
Swathed in bandages.

Curly Sam comes from down the street
Our garden a rough sort of place to meet
Girdling our prefab with dandelions and daisies
And above it all a skylark praises.
Christopher rides on his rusty three wheeler
Susan skates and swirls, a real crowd pleaser
Maureen skips, chanting loud
'Little fatty doctor, how's your wife?
Very well, thank you that's all right,
She can't eat a bit o' fish
Or a bit o' liquorice.
O.U.T spells.......
Sudden stillness, everything stops!
Two strange people glide along
Even the birds have stilled their song.
Two men like none we've ever seen
One with skin so black with glorious sheen
Tall as a giant with the straightest of backs
Carrying carpets, made into a sack.
The other as brown as treacle toffee, sweet
with an enormous hat and no socks on his feet.

Our hearts thudded, we all stood still
Eyes wide open and watched our fill.
Then the click of Maureen's gate, at the door they knock
Maureen's Mum stands there, speechless with shock
Then the bags are opened and rainbows revealed
As fabrics are flaunted , unfurled and unveiled.
Opulent organzas, shimmering silks
Purple satins, some white as milk,
Magenta and orange, turquoise and peach.
Maureen stretches her hand just to reach.
India and Africa have come to our street
Vibrant and vivid and warm and unique
Abundant, exquisite, exuberant and splendid
The world that was broken, might one day be mended.

Joyce Worsfold

Winking!

Mr. Wiffen walked in to the kitchen where we were sitting.
I saw his teeth.
His pink gums.
The whites of his eyes.
But the rest of him was black.
Completely black.
He seemed to be winking at me.
I asked my mum ;
'Why is Mr. Wiffen winking at me?'
Mum and Mrs. Wiffen laughed.
'He's not winking at you, son. He has just returned
home from the coal mine.
His eyes are still getting used to the light.
So that's why he seems to be winking.'

But I was not convinced.
He still seemed to be winking at me.
So I tried to wink back.
But I was not very good at winking
And Mr. Wiffen laughed at my efforts -
Uproariously!
After a while, he disappeared in to the bathroom for his daily soak.
He came back later,
a completely different looking man.
A white man!
And one who was no longer – *winking!*

Robert Taylor

Learning Light

The car was old, even then
Before most people dreamed of driving
An old Ford T, such majesty
With running boards and indicators
That flew out and flapped
There was no ignition key
But when it cranked, we clapped!

Oh it was old...
But not as old as grandma, Just automobile old
with fragrant leather seats and polished wood
Rusty not wrinkled
Every trip an adventure
Every journey was good.

Dad took us both, my brother and me
Right across the countryside towards the sea
Along lonely lanes and over bridges
Up endless hills and surprise view ridges
Car chuffing like an asthmatic old man
It gasped and stuttered then backward ran
Dad wrestled the handbrake and it jerked to a stop
And we jumped out like kangaroos, gave a skip and a hop.
Then...Dad let me steer while they both pushed
Right to the top and the whole world hushed.

And there below the whole earth lay
A green and gold jigsaw of hedges, flowers and hay.
'Let's watch!' said Dad in a voice full of awe
and Robert and I wondered what for?
Let's just sit and watch and see, all that there is and all that will be
We sat, in the silence. Waiting.

Waiting for what we didn't know
To catch the wind? The light? The glow?
Then somebody painted the sky
Handprints of scarlet, pink-madder and rose
Streamers of orange and ochre and gold
Invisible fingers stroked purple plains
Inky blue and violet stains
And behind it all there pulsed a great light
Layers and layers and layers of light.
Then the dark crept in, soundless and deep
And somewhere, in all that mystery
We fell asleep.

Joyce Worsfold

In the mirror

I remember you, we walked to school together
Hand in hand,
your tiny little hand in mine.
Remember the first day?
standing by mum's side, nervously, anxiously.
In case the teacher was a witch
Who would turn us into toads?
(Or even worse tadpoles!)

I remember you, they pinned a name on you,
A large white ticket round your neck,
Just in case you should forget who you were?
Oh, I remember you,
and the coke tips in the yard
Where Indians used to hide
and toy soldiers used to tire
when kerbstones became higher.

Oh, I remember you,
when the yard became much smaller.
When parents were shown to have faults!
And giants became teachers
(almost human!)
When beanstalks became trees and golden eggs began to burst.
And Jack emerged not quite so immortal.

I remember too,
Those dreams you carried in your back pocket
With the marbles, the conkers and the string
And the book of "Butterflies of Britain"
You stole from the school library.

I remember you,
In carpet slippers, in bewilderment, on the lawn,
Your hand in mine –
Little static folk in black and white,
So much changed,
So much gained,
So much lost.
Oh, I remember you,
I remember me.
I remember.

Robert Taylor

The Games of Life

Do you remember playing Hot Rice and kick-out ball
And ipsy gypsy on the garden wall
Could you roller skate a figure of eight
Or swing idly on the garden gate?
Do you remember when time was elastic
Before time-tables and tea breaks
Before business plans and strange new brands
Before mnemonics and abbreviations
Before mission statements and 'The Organisation'
Before Planning and aims
Do you remember when there were no 'objectives'
And the mountains were yours
And the valleys and plains
When the grass was head high
And the bracken was bigger
And you had invisible friends
 and a horse called trigger
When each day was a new adventure
And your identity was changed at will
You be the Indian and I'll be the cowboy
You be apache and me Buffalo Bill
You be Flash Gordon and I'll be the enemy
When did you get to be Mr. Pomposity?
When did you lose your great curiosity?
Did you have to grow up quite as much?
Did you have to deny the child
Lose your magic touch?
Can you bring back the wonder and why?
Can you lie on your back and consider the sky?
Can you look beyond it all?
For you're actually greater when you're small.

Joyce Worsfold

'I used to say that!'

We were waiting in the fish shop for the usual -
Whale sized fish, chips and mushy peas,
when this little girl in front of us in the queue, said to her mate;
'Shall we eat these in the factory par-cark?'
And her friend replied -
'Only if the Tare-caker, is not watching us!'

And I said;
'Par-cark? Tare-caker? I used to say that!'
And my wife said; 'I used to say that too!'
And I said; 'I didn't know that!'
And she said; 'Well, there you are,
there's **still** a lot you don't know about me!'

Then the man behind us in the queue,
With the pin striped suit and designer phone in his side pocket,
said in a posh voice-
'Par cark ? Tare-caker? I used to say that as well!'

And behind him in the queue, was an Hell's angel.
He had a leather jacket, rings in his ears,
dragons tattooed up each muscular arm.
He said;
'Par- Cark? Tare-caker? I used to say that all the time!'

And behind him in the queue,
was an old lady, with a kind face, a pleasant smile,
but hardly any teeth.
And she said ;
'Par-Cark? Tare-caker? That takes me back!'

Then the man behind the counter said;
'Look, does anyone want serving here, or what?'
And I said mischievously;
'Yes. *Chis and Fips* three times,
each *with pushy meas* on the side - Thank you very much.'
And everyone laughed, and said; '*I used to say that!*'

Robert Taylor

23

Saturday Matinee

I'm wearing my trusty gabardine
My brother has a Crombie overcoat
Some have blazers, some have no coats.
Shiny lace-ups, worn out plimsolls
Pounding pavements.
The kids are coming
The kids are coming
Strolling and bowling, bopping and running
No-one is dawdling, they all are a coming
From council house
And terraced row
Put-together prefabs
They all want to go.
To the Gaumont, Regal, Tivoli and Rex
Odeon, Palace, Playhouse and Ritz.

They're coming in hordes, gangs and huddles
Stepping over cracks, jumping in puddles.
Warm sweaty hands squeezing shillings
Slipping in sweet-shops all are willing.
Sherbet lemons, barley sugar sticks
Black-jacks that give us scary black lips
Aniseed balls, pear drops and jellies
Sweet confections to fill our bellies.
We ape grown-ups with sweet cigarettes
Anything sticky and gooey and wet.

A tidal surge of kids from every direction
Unaccompanied kids queuing in orderly fashion
Pay your sixpence, flood through the doors
Jump in dusty velvet seats, roll over the floors.
Pandemonium reigns, squealing and screeching,
Stamping of feet howling and hollering.
Usherettes bellow to some effect
Then spray each row liberally to disinfect!

Hush, the lights are dim and gutter
The curtain swags shimmy and stutter
Dust motes dance in projector beams
Hundreds of kids shuffle like jumping beans.
A crowing rooster tops some old weather vane
Heralding the mighty Pathe News again.
Then Bugs Bunny reigns or Pop-eye and Olive Oil
We giggle and chortle, guffaw and groan.
Then there is light, the intermission
And neatly capped ladies are on a mission

But soon are enveloped and besieged
As we lick, suck and slither vanilla ice-cream..

Words appear on the screen
And the majestic organ comes up through the floor
Some of us loll and some of us stand
And the music that sounds is vibrant and grand.
The cinema building vibrates with sound
Hit parade arias tumble around.
'Ma he's making eyes at me'
we all sing uncomprehendingly
then
'Gee but it's great after being out late
walking my baby back home'
Kids in pairs sashay forth and mime the actions
Borrowing combs and causing ructions.
They pretend to kiss and everyone snickers
And some swear rude words like 'bums' and 'knickers'.

The lights dim down for the main feature
We gaze and wait for some monster creature
What has happened to our mate Zorro
Last week trapped against spikes of horror,
We live it again, biting our nails
But he ducks in time and the sharp spikes fail,
Phew! That was a near disaster
But he's off again braver and faster.
OR
Ming the merciless waits for Flash Gordon
Holds him fast in an electric cordon
But I like it best when the Cisco Kid is riding
Galloping onwards lasso a flying
Cowboys and Indians fair lift the roof
With shouting and booing, I once lost a tooth.
We holler and hiss 'til our throats burn sore
And stamp fast our feet and clamour for more.

Then hurtling out into the light
We blink away unwelcome reality
And rearrange our coats the way we want to be
Flowing cloaks and flashing sabres
We gallop our horses through dangerous terrain
Where imagination is free to reign once again.

Joyce Worsfold

Fireworks Night

This year, once more,
We went to a bonfire night party,
In a town called Hexham,
thirty miles from where we live.
The fireworks were spectacular.
Lots of bright colours,
Incredible patterns,
Big bangs!
And the whole fantastically spectacular show went on for over half an hour!
An incredible advance on what fireworks were like when I was small.

Yet, watching it all,
I couldn't help remember
being a kid again.
The night, when we had not long moved into a new house,
on a new estate,
at Belle Isle, Leeds.
And all the neighbours had small children,
And everyone clubbed together to provide -
the food, the drink, the fire and the fireworks.
There were hot dogs
and hot potatoes
and parkin (ginger cake for those not in the know).
and every so often a firework to see......

'Right everyone, we are about to light The Roman Candle !'
'Woooooooooo!'
And five minutes later – 'This one is called Golden Rain!'
Five minutes later – 'Come on children - We've got a sparkler for everyone now!'
'Next, in two minutes, I'm going to light the Catherine Wheel. It's on a stick!'
'Wooooooo!'
And a little later.
'Stand back everyone - This one bangs- It's called a Jumping Jack.'
'Aaargh!!!!!! Oooh! Aragh! Whizz!'
'Right everyone here it is.....What we have all been waiting for. It's the most
expensive one in the box.The highlight of the night.- The Sky Rocket.'
'WWooooooooooooooooo!'
And up and up it went,
reaching for the stars, vanishing somewhere
near the far side of the moon.
Or so it seemed.
But then, everything seemed possible, in those far off unsophisticated days.

Robert Taylor

Strange incident at 460

Years ago,
When I was small,
And living in a *fairly new* house,
My dad arrived home from work,
hung his coat on a hook in the hall,
marched into the kitchen
and asked;
'Hello, darling, I'm home. What's for tea?'
He reached the kitchen
And stood face to face with a woman he knew- *slightly* -
But who wasn't his wife!
'Nothing for you,' She told him with a smile,
'because you don't live here!'
'Ah!' he said, laughing, but somewhat embarrassed.
'You're right. I don't!'
He went back into the hall,
Picked his coat off the hook,
And came home.............
'Hello, darling. I'm home.
Hee, you'll never guess what I've just done!'.....
Dad, was prone to tell tall stories.
But this was one was - *true!* .
Our *fairly* new neighbour - *two doors down* -
confirmed it the next day!

*P.S. Strange things happen when you live
in identical houses - two doors away from each other!!!!!*

Robert Taylor

Old Masters.

Heavy shears crunch cloth-
Barathea. Harris tweed.
Musk. Earth smell.
Dust.
Harry leans. His face intent.
Triangle of chalk
In nicotined fingers.
A flick of the wrist
Creates and indicates,
Folds, drapes, darts and tucks.

Machines orchestrate,
Playing cantatas with cotton spools,
Raucous voices raised –
"Music while you work."
Donald belts his hit parade –
"Because you're mine, the breezes hurry by,
Become a melody and I......"
Maisie in pinnie and turban
Croons as she feeds the presser foot,
"As long as he needs me."
-Worker's playtime.

You....sitting cross legged
On the table
Basting suits
Necklace of tape measure
And clicking thimble, singing,
"Mr Sandman, give me a dream....."

Hary cuts precisely,
Nip of waist
Swell of breast
Wing of bird ?
Patterns swing like flattened
Sides of beef.
Above his head –
"who do think you are? Christian Dior?"

Benny's bald head shines,
Metal framed specs, flushed face,
As he presides over the press.
Hiss of steam, scorched cloth
Knife pleats,
A lively whistle.

You survey your emporium,
Frustration, satisfaction,
A rush of orders to be met
And for you each must be
Absolute quality;
No frayed edges
No tangled stitch
No faults or puckers
They *must fit.*

This suit might talk at a treaty,
Feature in Pathe News,
Ride in a rolls,
Dance at the savoy.

Harry cuts,
Ben presses
 And you....you stitch and sing.
"I did it my way!"

Joyce Worsfold

The Boxing Glove

Discarded now
Bent, wrinkled and leathery
Body battered at the edges
Bits of you worn away by war and work,
Fatherhood, poverty and cigarettes.
As a youth you glowed like polished leather.
It fitted you then.
You danced lightly, sparring,
Muscles rippling, breathing regular.
Now you gasp for air
Your fight almost over.

Joyce Worsfold

Dad's Singing

We were walking along the front at Scarborough.
Dad was holding my hand.
I was nine years old.
It was Easter time.
It was very windy.
It was raining.
It was perishing cold.
The sea was crashing over the sea wall.
And -
Dad was singing very loudly.
'When the red, red robin comes bob, bob, bobbin' along.'
(I know! They don't write songs like that anymore!)

I implored him -
'Dad! Will you stop singing?'
'And he said, "Why? Don't you like that song?"'
And I said; 'No. Yes. It's just that people might hear you dad.'
I was just hoping that he would stop.
Instead - he sang a different song.

'Somewhere over the rainbow, skies are blue.'
And I looked up at the grey clouds and the rain.
And I said-
'Yes, somewhere a long way from here, dad!'
And he still kept singing.
I said; 'Dad! Please stop singing!'
And he said – 'Why?'
I said, 'because there's a family coming towards us.
And I think that *they* might hear you
and it's embarrassing!'
And he said; 'Okay.'
But he didn't stop singing.
He just - started singing - *another song.*

He sang.
'I believe, when every drop of rain that falls, a flower grows...'
And I said – 'That means there'll be a lot of flowers growing here dad, judging
by all this rain.'
And the family got nearer and nearer.
And I said; 'Please stop singing dad. That family will hear you.'
But *still* he kept singing -
'I believe that someone in the great somewhere,
hears every word.'
At which point, a giant wave crashed over the sea wall
and nearly knocked us off our feet.
We were soaked to the skin.

And the family approaching, stared open mouthed,
and then started laughing.
So, dad laughed too.
And so did I.
And Dad said – 'I told you that someone
 in the great somewhere hears every word. Didn't I?'
And I said- 'Yes, dad! He's heard every word.
And I think that - that - was *his* way of telling you to stop singing!'
And dad smiled. 'Hey, perhaps you're right.' He said.
And do you know what? - Dad stopped singing for
Oh .... *Five minutes at least!*

Robert Taylor

A mum with less brains!
(an overheard playground conversation)

Child 1: did you have a good weekend?

Child 2: Not really. I had to visit my mum in hospital.

Child 1: What's wrong with her?

Child 2: She's got to have her varicule brains removed.

Child 1: Her brains removed? What? All of 'em?

Child 2: No. Not all of 'em, stupid! She wouldn't be able to think would she,
     If she had all of 'em removed? No. It's just these varicule ones.
     Mind you, my mum's not very smart to start with. So I don't know how
     she'll go on with less brains than she's got now.'

Child 1: Oh, that's horrible. Poor you! Fancy having a mum with *less* brains!'

Robert Taylor

Tale of a Toilet

Teaching in nursery is always hectic
Sand for sick and antiseptic
Sand, sand, sand and mopping floors
Sorting toys and shutting doors.
Wiping paint and bums and noses,
finding shoes and spare clothes.
Supervising toilets and chivvying them on
Suddenly I hear this song...
'A place to pee, a place to pee
A toilet is a place to pee.'

Scott has time just to be
To wonder and to cogitate
To marvel and to meditate
and yes... to pee.
Not for him the rush and push,
The foolish haste, the adult rush
He has all the time in the world to enjoy ... a pee.
'Come on Scott we haven't all day
It's time for dinner
Wash your hands, collect your tray.'

Unfazed he smiles beautifically
Then eyes open wide shouts excitedly,
'My Mum sits down to pee
She doesn't stand up like me
And Miss, guess what, she hasn't got a tail'
Elisa, cross-legged starts to wail.
'I know, Scott' I cry.
He looks at me in great surprise.
'How do YOU know?' he loudly cries.

Joyce Worsfold

Boy Scout Camp

We sat, circling the camp-fire blaze
Domed by a deep dark summer sky
No walls enclosing
No roof, no doors
Just open-wide,
outside, out-numbered by stars.
And the boys?
Much horse-play and bandinage
Singing rude songs and fire-poking
Gathering sticks, laughing and joking.

Suddenly, silence, an unearthly glow
Seeps up behind the mountain slow
A momentous moon is rising
White-hot silver spilling
Slithering down mountains and molten on moors

A spotty, tousle-head strums a guitar
His face radiating freshness and fire-glow.
Above, starry space, voluminous and wide
Coruscated chambers ample and broad
The roly-poly moon globular and grand
Sails upward, rising our eyes on silvered strings
And then the stars begin to move
One pirouettes, pivots and spins across the sky
Carrying a tail of naked flame
Reeling, revolving and spinning
Across that great, grand plain
Shooting stars gyrating and wheeling
Have flown towards earth, stealing
For a few memorable moments
Amid rough and tumble, ruffle and rumpus
Of rowdy boy games
And left behind some sacred flames.

Joyce Worsfold

33

Cayton Bay

Some Friends of the family came round
with their daughter Jackie.
She was eleven - the same age as me.
All went well,
Until the family photograph albums came out.
Then I cringed.
No! Not those family albums.
"This is when we got married."
Alright - so far.
"This is when we were in the armed forces."
Alright - so far.
"This is when Joyce was born."
"Aw!"
(Joyce is my older sister).
There was Joyce in a cot,
 Joyce in a shawl,
Joyce on a mat,
Joyce in a pram,
Joyce at the seaside,
Joyce in the backyard.
Joyce, Joyce, Joyce, Joyce . . .

Then I was born.
Robert.
Robert in a cot,
Robert in a shawl,
Robert on a mat,
Robert in a pram,
Robert in the backyard
Robert with an ice cream on the front at Scarborough.
Robert, Robert, Robert, Robert.
Joyce and Robert,
Joyce, Mum and Robert,
Joyce, Dad and Robert.
(taken by someone who had cut off our heads!)
Joyce, two donkeys and Robert.

And then...it dawned on me what came next!

The next page was Cayton Bay!
We stayed at a caravan in Cayton Bay!

I was three when it was taken,
And oh! I curse the day,
Stood, stark naked, in a tin bath,
at a camp in Cayton Bay.

I didn't want Jackie to see it.
I didn't!
I didn't!
I didn't!
I had to get her out of there!
Out of the room, away from the photos.
I said, "Jackie! Would you like to come upstairs and play with my train set?"
Mum laughed and said,
"Don't be silly Robert. You haven't got a train set!"
"No," I said. "I mean, see my football game or Monopoly or something? Do you want to play those Jackie?"
She shook her head. She didn't want to play them.
I said, "Perhaps you'd like to go outside and
Play in the garden?"
"Don't be silly." Said Mum. "It's raining."
It was raining. But I was desperate by then.
When they turned over the page - she would see it.
She would see the photo.

I was three when it was taken,
And oh! I curse the day,
Stood stark naked in a tin bath,
at a camp in Cayton Bay.

I raced into the hall.
I was looking for something which would create a diversion.
A little something - which might send everyone dashing out into the hall.
I saw the telephone table
Complete with phone,
Phone book, address book, and magazines
and I kicked the table very hard.
Everything fell to the ground.
Clatter, clatter, clatter, clatter!
That should do it. But only Dad came out.
"What have you done now?" He said. "Pick it up-clumsy!"
So, I did -slowly.
The telephone, the phone books,
the address book and the magazines.

Then I went back into the front room and I heard…
Great Yarmouth,
Yarmouth, Yarmouth, Yarmouth,
Cornwall, Cornwall
Cornwall?.
Cornwall was when I was - well, at least - nine.
So, they'd leapt a few years and passed Cayton Bay.
Oh No! Jackie would have seen the photo.

Oh. No! Not the Photo!

I was three when it was taken,
And oh! I curse the day,
Stood stark naked in a tin bath,
at a camp in Cayton Bay.

I had to sit opposite Jackie
for the whole of teatime.
She kept smiling at me.
And I wasn't sure,
whether it was because she had seen the photo -
or because she was just being friendly . . .
But she kept *smiling at me.*
    And I was finding it hard to smile back.

The first chance I had,
I crept back into the front room,
found the photograph album
and I removed that photo.
I was not going to let anyone else see it.
Not that photo!
Oh no!

I was three when it was taken,
And oh! I curse the day,
Stood stark naked in a tin bath,
at a camp in Cayton Bay.

Robert Taylor

When I grow up

*'Now children, I wonder if you have thought about
What you'd like to be when you grow up.*

Yes, Thomas, what would you like to be?'
'Well I'm 8 now and I've given it a lot of thought
And I reckon I've got 2 choices.
Either I could be a postman
But I'd have to do it on a bike
I can't drive you see,
OR
I could be an ice-cream man.
I think that's the one I'd really like to be
But I'd have to be very careful
And ration myself to say, two or three
And only on a very hot day.
Otherwise it wouldn't pay.

What about you, Abigail?
'I'd like to be a best man when I grow up
I saw one at a wedding,
Everyone seemed to like him and laughed and clapped a great deal
And afterward you have a meal
With cheesecake and wine and sausages on sticks
And I'd like all that, and I'm good at funny bits
When my Mam said you have to be a man to be one, I cried
But maybe, perhaps I'll be a bride.'

'Now, Ryan I'm sure you've got lots of ideas'
Well, my Dad thinks I should be an architect
'Cos I'm good at drawing plans
I drew some for the rabbit hutch
For me Grandad up at me nans
An architect is posher, than a plumber like me Dad
But I'd rather be a plumber and my Dad does drive a Jag!

'And what about you Michael, you're sitting up very nicely.'
I'd like to be a dinner lady
But my Mum says I can't
Apparently you have to be a woman… and I aren't
But best of all I would be a cigarette roller
I saw a man doing it once and II never saw ought cooler
He had this little machine, and tiny paper sheets
And some tobacco, he also had big feet.
'Now, Wayne, what's your ambition?
When I grow up I'm going to drive a lorry
It will be ginormous

And anyone who gets in the way will be sorry.
And you have a bed in the back for taking naps
And a fridge for your beer and stuff
Only thing is I'm not right sure about reading maps
Books are absolutely bad enough

'Joanne, do you have some special dreams?'
Actually, I'm going to be a strong man
'Do you mean a strong woman?
'No! I'm going to be a strong MAN
I've been practising a lot, lifting tins of beans
They build your muscles really strong
AND I do press-ups...but not for long

Rachel, what would you like to do?
Well, we went on a school visit to a hotel place
There were maids and laundry people all over't space
Receptionists, waitresses and porters too
There were a lot of jobs there to do
The personnel officer said, quite a few
But she kept going on about business-men
And suddenly, then... I really got cross
I mean why is it men who get to be boss?
'Excuse me' says I, 'Don't business women stay here'
She went quite pink and said 'Oh yes, quite a few this year
And it is estimated that by the year 2010
Fifty percent of our executives will be women.'
I smiled, because it's very plain to see
That one of them, definitely will be me!

Joyce Worsfold

38

A Cat In School

A family friend, Lillian, told me this story about when she was a young school girl in Liverpool.......

I always sat at the back of the class room,
But I always *tried* to listen carefully to what my teacher told me to do.
One day, the teacher, Mrs. Lewis, asked us all to bring a ca......t into school.
I wasn't certain, but I *think* she said - cat!
I thought, a cat would make an exciting lesson.
We could draw it, describe it and all sorts.
So, that night I told my mum.

    'Mum! Mrs. Lewis wants us to take a cat into school tomorrow.'
    'A cat? A cat! Why on earth would she want you to take a cat into school?'
    'I don't know,' I said. 'To draw -and things.'
    'Ah, well. We haven't got a cat,' she said, 'So, you're out of luck there.
Mind you, you could try next door. Mrs Connor's got four cats. Perhaps she'll let you borrow one of hers.'

    So, I went next door to Mrs. O' Connor. I told her about needing a cat for school and she said.

    'A cat? A cat! Why on earth would you want to take a cat into school?'
    'I don't know.' I said. 'To draw and things.'
She finally agreed to let me borrow one of her cats. But she said -

    'I wouldn't take Henry. He scratches.
And I wouldn't take Hilda, she bites.
While Maisey can be bad tempered and spits.
If I was you, I'd take Jamie, he's friendly and good natured. Mind you, you'll have to catch him first. He is very - *quick!*'

    The next morning, I was at Mrs O ' Connor's house nice and early to catch the cat.

    Henry and Hilda were no where to be seen. Jamie, indeed, proved to be too fast to catch. He escaped down the garden, so we were left with the bad tempered, spitty one - called Maisey.

    She was fast asleep in a chair.
    'Oh well.' Mrs. O' Connor said. 'beggars can't be choosers, I suppose. Maisey it is.'

    We got her into a basket and closed the door. I promised to look after her. I carried her all the way to school and she didn't wake up once.

    Mind you, I was most surprised to find that I was the only one who had remembered to bring a *cat.*
Everyone else had brought a boring old – *carrot* instead!

Robert Taylor

Playground Duty

Children
Careering around the playground
Hopping and jumping
Wailing and howling and tigging and thumping.
Me, standing still
Eyes roaming about
Aware of each huddle, each game and each shout
When away to my left
My eyes catch a sight
That sets my heart beating
Something is in flight.
A bevy of balloons?
All gently floating
And twenty ten year olds, giggling and gloating
Can it be? Can it be?
Do my eyes deceive me
I must send for the head
She will never believe me
Hundreds of CONDOMS blown up and flying
All around the estate, ducking and diving
Some full of air and some full of water.
They could have prevented some son or some daughter
But now they are free from their hiding places
And some Mums and Dads will have very red faces.
And whom shall we punish, at whom shall we shout
Who caused the condoms to be thrown all about?

At the end of break I went to the Head Teacher
She was a 'born again spinster'
How could I reach her
Would she understand what I had to relate
The rest of the staff could hardly wait
'In the playground,' I mumbled 'The children have condoms'
A bit hard of hearing she thought I said pom-poms
'Well it's not something about which you need bother me
Let them sew them on hats and just let me be.
You could sew two together to make little birds
Write the alphabet on them and let them make words,
You know dear, we must use every resource we can find,
to educate children, to develop their minds.
Now back to your classroom
Or there'll be a riot
And work with the pom-poms, in peace and in quiet.'

Joyce Worsfold

A Colossal Thing!

I'll never forget 'what's-his-name.'
I sat next to him in class -
in junior school.
We were always having a laugh.
(Well, one of us was!)
Brain-box was his middle name.
(I don't remember the rest!)
First up his hand,
first out with the answer.

In maths?
'A rhombus sir!'

In history?
'Six wives sir. And he beheaded two'

In geography?
'Mt. Kilimanjaro, sir. And Ben Nevis in Britain.'

See. Bright as a button. –
And twice as clever.

Me? I was still struggling with the countries of the British Isles.
I knew that there were five.
But for some reason - I kept forgetting - *Eire.*
Well, that and - *long division.*

However, the one thing that I could match him at
Was - spelling.
I don't know why.
And once he cheated in the weekly spelling test.
He asked *me* how to spell a word.
The word was - *colossal.*
'Is it two L's or two S's?' he whispered, out of the corner of his mouth.
And I like a fool answered.
'Two of each,' I told him, out of the corner of mine.
'But only the esses are together.'
He laughed at my cleverness.

And -
I got *a gold star* that week,
for getting twenty out of twenty.
Only one other child in the class,
got twenty out of twenty that week.

He did.

What's-his-name. Thing-a-my-bob. Brain-box.
Except, he got *two gold stars* instead of the one.
The other star was for - *neatness.*
Huh! Boy! Did that make me angry!

What made me angrier still, was that some children,
sat behind us in class - accused me of cheating!
They said that they *had heard- me - ask him-*
how to spell - Colossal!

And what was even *worse, was that, he just sat there grinning –*
letting them believe *that it was true!*

Yes, I remember, 'What's-his-name,'
'Thing-a-me-bob.' 'Brainbox.'

He went to grammar school.
I didn't!
He passed A levels.
I didn't!
He became an accountant.
I didn't!
He went to live in those posh houses on the edge of town.
I didn't!
But did *he know how to spell - Colossal?*

.....................*I did!*

Robert Taylor

42

Can we write us news?

Can we write us news
Miss! Can we do us news?
I've summat to write about
Can we choose?
Last night I was sick in bed
All over't covers
There were bits of green and red,
So I went to get in with me Mam
But Uncle Bill was there,
So I slept with our Sam!.

'On Saturday we watched the tele
Zorro was on and Tarzan and we 'ad thee bowls of jelly,
Six packets of crisps and some of Dad's beer
But he don't know 'cos he wasn't there.'

On Sunday me Dad said, 'Come for a ride'
We went to this 'ouse and he went inside,
This lady drew curtains and he stayed about an 'our
The he gave me a quid and said, 'money's power'

Last night my Dad went to the Royal Oak
Me Mam was mad 'cos she said we was broke.
Anyway, he brought 'ome a bird
And me Mam got mad as mad as could be
And . . . It were a pheasant and we 'ad it for tea.'

'Last night me and my Dad went pinching lead,
I nearly fell and me Dad he said,
Be careful, lad just how you perch.
Especially when we're on a church!'

This morning it was hawful in hour house
'Cos when we went to the toilet, there was this little mouse
Then we had no toilet rolls, not even one
So me Mam had to cut up yesterday's Sun,
She said, 'That's what you do when you're poor'
Then she hung it on a string on a nail on the door.'

On Sunday I was sad because my Grandad died
Me Mam told us and we all cried
He was my very favourite relation
But me Gran's all right
She's got an alsation'
We 'ad spaghetti last night
It were proper stuff not out of a tin

And when you tried to eat it it wouldn't go in
Me Mam said she'd had it many times
But I didn't like it I'd rather have Heinz.'

Our budgie died this morning,
Me Dad said, 'We'll cremate it'
So he threw it on't fire
But the cat jumped up and ate it.'

'Last yesterday I watched, 'News at Ten'
There was this fella reading it sat under Big Ben
You can now get babies in a test tube
I think it's better, the other way's rude!'

Miss, Miss, can we do us news
I've summat to tell thee
Can we choose?
Miss can you spell it for me
Cos I don't know how and I want to tell it to thee.'

Miss, I aint got any news to tell
We never do nothing
Life's boring as hell!

Joyce Worsfold

Children like me.

I wish . . . I wish . . . I wish . . .
I wish I wasn't me.
I wish I was him, or her, or it, or them.
I wish I had a far off secret den.
I wish I was Megan, or Sophie and Jen.
(Anyone but me!)

I wish I was important, or good at sums,
wonderful on guitar, piano or drums.
I wish I got on with my dad and my mum.
(All we seem to do is argue!)

I wish it wasn't my turn to wash the pots,
I wish I hadn't sat all day in wet socks.
I wish I could wear trousers and casual tops.
(Instead of school uniform!)

I wish my legs weren't short and fat.
I wish my ears didn't stick out like that.
I wish my chest wasn't quite so flat.
(I hope it's going to happen soon!)

I wish Tony Clayton would notice me.
I wish my mum would quit nagging occasionally.
I wish it wasn't the morning, but half past three.
(Time to go home again!)

I wish it wasn't today we had that science double,
I wish my teacher's beard was designer stubble.
I wish I hadn't spoken out and got into trouble.
(Another detention again!)

I wish I was a model modelling clothes,
or a famous footballer scoring goals.
I wish I could wake up with a smaller nose!
(And get rid of all my freckles and spots!)

I wish I wasn't here, but there,
anywhere - but this school chair.
Except for parts of Africa - I'm glad I'm not there.

We saw this film -
Children like me only . . . thinner.
Children like me only . . . sadder.
Children like me only . . . homeless.

Children like me only . . . orphaned.
Children like me only . . . starving.
Children like me only . . . *dying.*

I'm glad I'm me and not them.
I'm glad I'm here and not there.

It's not that bad - being me.
Sometimes - I suppose.

Robert Taylor

Bones!
(A conversation with my son at four years old.)

'Daddy! Have you got bones in your body?'
'oh yes. I've got bones.'
'Like ....dinosaurs have bones?'
'Mm, yes. But Dinosaurs had much bigger bones- Most of them.'
'Do all daddy's have bones?'
'Yes. All daddy's have got bones.'
'And mummy. Does mummy have bones.'
'Oh yes. All mummy's have got bones.'
'And do – Do houses have bones?'
'Oh, no. they have wooden frames - Most of them.'
'Do cars have bones?'
'No not cars. Cars are made of metal and plastic.'
'Does Sheila have bones?'
'Sheila? You mean your dinner lady at school?'
'Yes.'
'Well, I expect she will have - Almost certainly.'
'And Mrs. Hetherington. – will she have bones?'
'Oh yes. Your teacher will have bones."
'And even Mrs Joyner too - The Head Teacher?'
'Oh yes. All teachers have bones!'
'What? All teachers?'
'Yes.'

'Urrghhhh!'

Robert Taylor

Saturated

It was the way she told the stories
Leaving them like lozenges to be sucked on,
Savoured, swallowed
Lick by lick.
The stories became part of them
All thirty-six of them
Princess by princess
Forest and king.

Long, long ago, in a lost kingdom
Just left of the National Curriculum
and before directed time.
There were days to wallow
neck deep in story.
Bones were marrowed in poetry,
Imaginations elasticated in play.
Children counted on and counted back
Through a labyrinth
Testing out hypothesis
beginning life at Genesis and ending with a revelation.

She guided them as they danced through their stories
Pencils flying unfettered,
Then re-drafted, jig-sawed into shape.
Confident as authors, publishing day-dreams.
There were hours each week for reading
Curled on cushions foetally, thumbs in mouths.
Soaking in Sewell, dripping in Dahl,
Hans Anderson and Grimm.
Grabbing at fantasies
Gulping magic.
She had time to hear them read.

This term she planned,
Examined
Assessed
Dissected
Studied reams of dried out paper,
Put ticks in all the right boxes…

And shattered into fragments!

Joyce Worsfold

47

School Theatre Visit

Scrubbed faces, eyes alight
'Got me new dress on, Miss, in honour o't night.'
'Eh, Miss you don't 'alf look nice
Me Mam's got same coat from't catalogue
But we ain't got to tell me Dad the price.'

Bags bulging with galactic delights,
Mars Bars and Milky Ways, Galaxy's held tight.
Pregnant pockets jingling
Excited chatter mingling
Shined shoes a clattering
as the coach arrives.
Forty little legs all head for the rear,
'We gorrit first! I were foggy!'
'Gerrout of 'ere!'
'You've got to sit in front with Miss
'cos you're always sick,
she likes the sick ones next to her
so she can be quick!'
Heads counted and I say 'Sit down!' a million times
And indicate with sour looks and exaggerated mimes.
'Ooh look at motorway, we're going over now
Look there's a sheep up there, or is it a cow?'
'Miss is it true that cows make yoghurts
'Cos me Dad says they do?
Do they born 'em like babies or make 'em like stew?'

'Eh, look at that castle, aint it big
Is it Windsor, Miss or't palace o't Queen?
It's the only castle I've ever seen.'
'That's no castle, it's Armley Gaol,
Me Dad's in there, I've been it's REAL!'
Town hall next. 'Miss look at them lions.'
'Miss, Wayne's pinched me Smarties
And now he's got Brian's.'
'Is that we're we going? 'Cor look at that golden ball

and them golden owls, it says 'Civic Hall.'
Coach stops amid mayhem and strife
And each disgorges it's pulsating life.
Teachers shepherd, cajole and shout
gesticulating wildly as they get their charges out.
Up the steps and all in a muddle,
'Keep in twos now there's no need to cuddle.
Simon, NO! That's not our group
Peter don't do that... why did you bring a flask of soup?

It's all right, Tracey, it will wash out,
It's a nice shade of orange
There was no need to clout!
Don't run up those stairs or else you'll fall
Well I told you Sam, you're no rubber ball.'
In seats at last and counting heads
36,37, no that's not mine, it's Fred's.
'Fred I've got one of yours, three of mine are missing.
'Oh toilets of course!'
I trek down the stairs yet again
With Melanie and Martin, but no sign of Ben.
Back up the stairs and Ben has been sick
Right over the balcony, oh he is thick!
Better find a mop and sand and a cloth
I dart around like a neurotic moth.

Suddenly the lights are dimmed
The curtain raised at last
And I sink into my seat
And forget what just has passed.
I don't view the stage very much at all
Just each one of their faces,
Alight with wonder and suddenly so small.
The witch is so scary and cruel
The clown is so funny, an absolute fool,
The wizard all horrid and the princess all good
And who knows what monsters are alive in that wood?

Magic everlasting, the theatre still thrills
in a world full of tele, videos and pills.
They clap and they stamp and shout fit to burst
then clamour for ice-cream
and drink, not just to quench thirst.
Ices dispensed and litter picked up
I'm dead on my feet, smell coffee, dream of a cup.
Still, here is my lolly, now isn't that funny
Selina has sat on it and now it's all runny.
'Don't cry, Selina, your bottom will dry,
you're better off than me, I'm thirsty fit to die.'

Lights dim again, back to the enchanted land
Frightened sticky fingers catch hold of my hand
Then it's all over, they clap 'til their sore
'twas an awful production but they'll never know.
Back on the coach sleepy heads roll
Tousled heads, close together,
curled up in a ball.
Arms and fingers close-entwined,

Sticky thumbs in sticky mouths
No-one left behind.

'Wake-up, Simon, Mummy's here.'
'Wayne here's Daddy!' (Oh! He reeks of beer)
Ben and Sandy, Melanie too.
'Andrew, wake-up, Grandad's come for you.'
39, 40 all but two have gone.
Doesn't look like they're coming
Better take them home.
Drive around the narrow streets
Looking for Mum
She's out, let's try Auntie and failing that Gran.

At last they're safe, tucked up in their homes
asleep in their beds, dreaming of witches and gnomes.
But as I take my leave I hear a whispered aside,
'Yer know them teachers have a reet bobbies job
They don't have to pay for ought you know,
free seats at theatre and free on't coach they go
and all they do is take a few kids to some theatre show.'

Joyce Worsfold

Chinese Whispers

Pretty Su-ling in a silk cheongsam
Waits for the love of a beautiful boy
He drives a moped in Vietnam
She cooks clams and delicious doughboy

Joyce Worsfold

Towards Plain English

My teacher said;
'You've been skating on thin ice, my boy!'
I said;
'I haven't been near any ice, sir!'
He said;
'You're sailing far too close to the wind.'
I said;
'Sailing, sir?'
He said;
'Don't try to pull the wool over my eyes.'
I said
'What wool, sir?'
And he said;
'Now boy, you're up the creek, without a paddle and no mistake!'
And I said;
'A creek, sir? But I haven't been near any creek!'
And he said;
Don't try and deny it, boy. You see, I keep my ears close to the ground.'
And I said;
Well, I didn't know what to say!
But he said;
'You've been caught red handed, boy!
And this time, this time you've got your fingers burnt!'
I said;
'Eh?'
He said;
'Pardon! The word is pardon boy! Not 'eh''
And I said;
'Pardon, sir. Pardon?'
And he said;
'That's better, Hoskins.
But don't you think it's about time you pulled up your socks'
(So I did)
'And rolled up your sleeves'
(So I did)
'Put your elbows in to it!'
'Into what, sir?'
'Kept your nose to the grindstone?
And worked your fingers to the bone?'
'Yer what, sir?'
'It's pardon, boy. Pardon!
Don't you understand *Plain English?*'

Robert Taylor

51

A Choice of Careers

'What do you want to be when you grow up son?'
'I want to be a cow, dad. Grazing in pasture, idly chewing grass by slow moving
streams.
And serenity appeals to me.'

'Well, have you thought about electronics-
Or plastics! There is a lot going on in the world of plastics!'

'I'd like to be a cloud, dad - drifting gently in the sky. No feelings. No worries.
No chance of being hurt.
And drifting appeals to me.'

'Tell me, have you thought about the civil service - or computer programming?
Or maybe.....teaching?
There must be something you can do.'

'I could be a seashell, dad.
On a lonely pebbled beach,
talking to seaweed and starfish.
Delighting other children with my -
'Can you hear the sea noises?'
And sea noises appeal to me.'

'But son, I'm impatient.
And so is your mother.
You've got your degree.
And son - you're *twenty five already!*
So, please make up your mind.'

Robert Taylor

52

'Being shown the ropes!'

Dad owned a small clothing factory in Leeds.
I went to work for him and he 'showed me the ropes.'
Pretty soon, I was sewing buttons on jackets by machine,
putting buttonholes in,
 working in the office doing the books in a morning
and working as 'Head passer,' in the afternoons.
(actually, I was the only passer! Except for my dad, who constantly and
meticulously checked over my work!)

One day, he took me into Leeds city centre
And we visited a very well known gents outfitting shop.
Dad - took various suits off the rack and held them up so that I could appraise
them and pick out any mistakes or defects.
Together we noticed -
Cotton hanging from several pockets......
Shine on a jacket breast which shouldn't be there......
A lapel with stitches missing....
A jacket where one lapel was slightly shorter than the other....
I did not spot that one - but he did.
There was a *quarter of an inch* difference between the two lapels.
He measured them with the tape measure he always kept in his jacket pocket.
He was a professional and he could see the *quarter of an inch difference* with
the naked eye.
 'All these faults should have been checked and eliminated long before they
reached the shop.' He informed me.
'What, even the quarter of inch difference on the lapels?' I said disbelievingly.
'Most people wouldn't notice that dad!'
'But I would!' He snapped back. 'And any professional should.'

He picked up a rather expensive suit. Read the price tag on the ticket
and winced.
'Dear me,' He said. 'Look at the price of that? Good material but I'm not
sure the finish matches it.'
He took the jacket off the hanger, put his hand inside it and held it up.
'Tut! Tut! Look at that sleeve. Can you see what's wrong with it?'
'It's hanging too far forward dad!' I told him triumphantly.
'Yes,' he said. 'Far-too-far-forward. They should have spotted this in the factory.
The other sleeve is hanging okay. But – hang on! Just look at that stitching on
the sleeve, right there - where it meets the shoulder. It's appalling.'
It was too.
'A faulty sewing machine that.' He went on. 'It should never have got through
the factory. It's dreadful! In fact, I bet if I held up this jacket and tugged at that
sleeve, it would probably come clean away from the shoulder.'
'Yes, dad. But you won't do it will you?' I asked nervously.
There was a wicked twinkle in dad's eye. I had seen it before - a worrying
twinkle.

'Well, I might.' He said. 'It is bad workmanship and it's what it deserves.'
He held up the jacket, and as I gasped in total disbelief.
He gave the sleeve one almighty tug.
As he predicted, the sleeve did come clean away from the rest of the jacket.
My mouth dropped open. I suddenly wished the ground would open and swallow me up.
A young shop assistant arrived and asked dad.
'Can I be of assistance sir?'
'Yes.' Dad replied without flinching, draping the jacket with only one sleeve, over one of the young assistant's arms.
'You can send this rubbish back to your factory – It's a reject!'
The assistant's astonished look was unforgettable.
'Oh, and so is this sleeve!' dad added. Draping that over the assistants other arm.

'Come on lad,' He said to me. 'We're leaving. I won't be buying anything in here ever again!'
And dad was right. I personally, *dare not go near the shop ever again!*
In fact, whenever I walked passed that particular shop – my pace quickened!
Even when the shop was – CLOSED!!

Robert Taylor

The Cat with 2 P's.

It was my second year in teaching.
His name was Herbert.
He was seven years old.
He asked me for a word.
His word book was open at the letter N.

I said ; 'Yes, Herbert. What word would you like?'
And he said – 'Nibstrobe!'
Well, it sounded like - Nibstrobe!
'Did you just say; Nibstrobe?' I asked.

'No! Nipstrome!' he replied somewhat indignantly.
'Oh!' I said. 'Did you say, Nipstrome!'

'No!' he said. 'Nipstrum!'
'Right. Nipstrum?' I said, still not getting it.

He smiled. 'Yes, Nipstrum.' He added. 'That's the word I want.'

I had to ask…..'What - what is - a Nipstrum, Herbert?'

He gave me this look. A look that said ;
'Call yourself a teacher and you don't know what a Nipstrum is!'

He crossed his arms in disgust and said -
'It's my cat's name of course!'

I laughed and said – 'Of course it is Herbert. I ought to have known!'

Then I wrote the word down for him in his word book.
I wrote - N - I - P - S - T - R - U- M.

He stared at what I'd written and said ;
'Aw! You've spell it wrong, Mr! It's got two P's and you've only spelt it with one!'

I corrected it of course and told him.
'Oh well, I'll know next time!'

Then I wrote in my school diary -
'Please note -*Nippstrum is a cat with two P's!'*

Robert Taylor

55

Robert's Train

Bare floors has Robert's house
And you wouldn't sit on the chairs
The whole place smells of urine
There are jagged holes in the stairs.

'Santa's gonna bring me a train, Miss
electric with loads of rails
and engines that pull all the carriages
It'll be bigger and better than Dale's.'

Dale says 'I've got loads of engines
and trucks that carry real coal
But Wayne's got bridges and tunnels
You can watch them come out of the hole'

Robert's knees hang out of his trousers
The soles on his shoes flap about
And his coat . . . well he hasn't got one
He's a tough little lad when he's out.

'Santa's gonna bring me a train, Miss
It'll go right fast an all
Santa's gonna bring me a train Miss
I'll draw a picture to put on the wall'

His Mum dances topless twice nightly
His Dad live three streets away
'He's Dale's Dad now,' he says brightly
'Santa will come on his sleigh!'

Christmas is lovely in my home
The tree stands sparkling and tall
The table is laden with goodies
And brightly wrapped presents for all
But as I serve Christmas dinner
Part of me fills with pain
An ache in my heart keeps returning
And one thought keeps filling my brain
'When Robert woke up this morning
Had Santa left him a train?'

We returned in the new year
And the children wrote all their news
Robert was quiet, not writing
But I noticed a new pair of shoes.
'I got a watch, Miss'

He said proudly, holding his arm up high

I looked at the watch with interest
My lips ready forming a reply
'But Robert, the hour hand's missing'
I said with a sinking heart
'I know' said Robert rapidly blinking
'But the big hand tells me a part,
I know when its quarter to something
I know when it's quarter past
And Santa, he brought it for me
And I didn't even ask!'

Joyce Worsfold

Compost

They say if you pee in a compost bin
The loam is made the quicker
The chemical surge
Is made to purge
the contents to something richer.
It used to be thought in days gone by
that a bishop's pee was best.
But now we know
It is not so
Science has done the test.
Though men can pee further
And it generally is stronger.
All pee is equal it's true
So the soil that comes from a compost bin
Is largely up to you.

Joyce Worsfold

Timothy's Arm

Timothy was born
with only one arm
He arrived in school and caused a furore
with a hooked appendage that he used for his glory.
Captain Hook he played with fervour and speed
He was the hero of all daring deeds
The one who was blessed with great admiration
The one who could cry with loud indignation

'Me write a story
With only one arm?
You must be joking
I'll just play with the farm
With Meccano and Lego and then with the cars
With the rocket that races right up to the stars
With the sand and the water and then with the bricks
But I can't do no work with only this stick!
So don't lose your temper, just keep calm
I'm just a little lad with only one arm.'

One day Tim arrived with a tremendous new toy
An electronic arm with fake fingers was his special joy
He had it for all of the days of one week
And all of his mates queued up for a peek
Then he went to Scarborough sands
When filling the bucket he had, yes, two hands!
He dug and he patted his sandcastles out
And ran into the sea with a gleeful shout
The waves which he jumped tumbled and crashed
And Timothy happily giggled and splashed
But somehow the tide it took it's toll
As it sucked at flotsam and billowed and rolled
And away on the tide, away safe from harm
Floated the expensive Timothy's arm.

Some months later he was given another
And told to take care by his militant mother
He had a go at dressing for games and P.E
He swung from the wall bars shouting, 'Hey look at me'
He tried drawing and painting and even some writing
And at home with his brothers, wrestling and fighting
At the end of the day he went peacefully to bed,
First making sure that the Rottweiler was fed.
Late in the night the dog fancied a bone
And took it to the garden and into its home,
But oh in the morning, Timothy cried

When his mangled arm in a hole he espied.
The dog was an alien and lost all it's charm
The night that it ate most of Timothy's arm.

Another arm, it was decided
should be kept in school, carefully guarded
Each night it stood in state upon a battery charger
Ceremoniously put in place by the special needs teacher
Every night it glowed, green in the gloom
A sinister presence, in the head-teacher's room.
Until,....
One night a burglar came with stealth
Dreaming of unheard of wealth
He crawled the corridor to avoid the alarm
And came face to face with.... Timothy's arm!
With its fingers splayed in a threatening palm
The burglar ran terrified by Timothy's arm.

Timothy grew and changed many lives
With his mischievous make-up and twinkling eyes
One day he will do all that any man can
For Timothy's arm is part of... a wonderful plan!
For technology can make for us all
Replacement bits when age comes to call.

Joyce Worsfold

ABC poem

A rippled pond reflects a mackerel sky
Burnished and gleaming like polished plate
Cool and placid, convoluted and green
Dreaming damp.
Endowed abundantly with submerged life.
We see only surface innocence.

Joyce Worsfold

Oh! For a quiet life.

It was the run up to Christmas and as a very young teacher, not too long in the job, I was feeling very fraught and frazzled.
My class of 35 year fours contained 28 boys and 7 girls.
A very unusual balance – and boy, were they noisy!
I am convinced that several of the boys would have made excellent foghorns!
They could have been foghorns for England!

I had to admit, I was counting down the days until Christmas!

One day in assembly, the deputy head, was telling a story to the whole school.
For some reason, I found his story attractive. It went like this......

"If a person described his life as being -
'Like walking through a meadow full of flowers,
On a bright sunny day, with an endless blue sky overhead and butterflies fluttering
And bees buzzing and birds singing and not another sound to be heard anywhere.'

What sort of life do you think that person would have had?"

Several hands went up amongst the assembled throng of children.
The deputy head picked a boy called Darren.

"Yes, Darren?"

"A boring one, sir."   Said Darren.

The deputy head, obviously taken by surprise, laughed.
Several teachers smiled and their mouths dropped open – including mine.

It wasn't *quite* the answer - *we* had *in our* heads!

Robert Taylor

60

Can anybody here do this sum?

I was a young teacher in my second year of teaching. The Head Teacher announced at the weekly staff meeting, that he had heard that there were school inspectors in the area.

'If one visits our school,' he said, 'I'll try to send round a warning notice. I shall draw a black spot, on a plain piece of paper and send it round school with a child.'

A few days later, on a Monday morning, George, the teacher in the next classroom, said to me before school assembly,

'Well, I wonder if we'll get that black spot today?'

'I don't know.' I said. 'let's hope not!'

'Well,' he said laughing loudly. 'Best be prepared lad. Best be ready.'

Then he winked and went to his classroom.

As soon as assembly ended and my class were filing back into my classroom, a child with a piece of paper arrived. It was a child from George's class. I opened the paper and it was blank. Blank! - Except for a black spot – smack in the middle of the page. My immediate reaction was that George had sent it, as a joke.

I wrote on the bottom of the paper; 'You'll not get me with that one George.'

I folded the paper, handed it back to the child and sent him on his way, and smiled to myself.

A couple of minutes later, I was smiling no more. A tall, severe looking gentleman, with horned rimmed glasses and a clipboard entered my classroom and said.

'Mind if I watch your lesson, Mr, mm, Taylor?'

And then, without waiting for a reply, made his way to the back of my classroom and sat down, clipboard at the ready. Trying not to panic, I settled my class down and announced.

'Right everyone, today we are going to carry on with the Subtraction skills we started on Friday.' I pointed to one of the sums I had written on the blackboard and said;

'Now then, who would like to do this sum for us?'

Several hands shot up.

'Yes, Andrew, would you like to have a go for us?'

'Please, Mr Taylor, can I go to the toilet?'

'Well, not really Andrew, we have just started our lesson. Didn't you go straight after assembly?'

'No. Mr Taylor. I did not want to go then. But I do now'

Andrew, stood up, holding himself, and hopping up and down. I feared a puddle on the floor.

'Alright, Andrew, but be quick and be sure to wash your hands afterwards. Right now, who would like to do the sum for us?'

Lots more hands went up and I picked Julie.

'My Grandad died this weekend Mr.Taylor.'

'Oh, I'm sorry to hear about that. Your family must be terribly upset.'

'Oh yes. But my gran's still alright. She's still got a parrot and a Pekinese.'

'Oh, right, but . . . '

'North and South' She added.

'I beg your pardon.....'

'Her pets are called North and South. The parrot is called North because he lives high up in a cage. And the Pekinese is called South because he lives down on the ground.'

'I don't get it!' said Claire.

61

'Me neither said Debra.'

'I do !' said Peter, 'It's because North is.....'

'Well, they are very clever names.' I said. 'We'll talk more later. But let's get back to our sums. Can anybody do this sum?'

'I had a gerbil that died once!' Joanne said.

'I had a cat which got run over by a truck!' said David. 'And I had a pet rat!'

'Yes, well that's enough of that David. Can we please get back to our sum. Now who would like to do it for us?'

Several children put up their hands. I chose Sarah.

She began. 'Do you like cake with flies in Mr Taylor?'

'You mean, wedding cake?'

'Yes. My mum got married on Saturday.'

'Your Mum!' I said, taken by surprise. "So, was it a good do?'

'Oh Yes. But not as good as *my dad's* wedding last week.'

'Oh! Well, very nice. We'll talk about that later too. Now can anybody here do this sum?'

A few of the children put their hands up. I picked Jonathan this time. He was the best at maths in the whole class.

'Right, Jonathan. Will you do the sum for us?'

'Sir! Someone's written shit on my desk!' He replied.

'Someone's done what?'

'Written shit on my desk!'

'Well,' I said. 'Go get a cloth from the sink and wipe it off then!'

'I can't! I can't! It's scratched on!'

Wayne, sat at the next desk leaned across and added his four penny worth.

'It may have been scratched on with one of those compasses we use for drawing circles.'

I was wondering, if this was a confession and that Wayne had scratched the word on in the first place. But I could hardly accuse him there and then.

'Right. We will get to the bottom of this later.' I said. 'Now can we please go on with the lesson.'

However, Jonathan crossed his arms and stamped his feet. It was very uncharacteristic of him.

'I'm not sitting here with shit on my desk! He yelled. 'I'm not! I'm not! I'm not!'

I got him to swap places with Wayne. Wayne did not seem to mind moving.

But there was more tension because Danielle, who was now set next to Wayne objected to him being there - something about a family feud. I told her, quietly, that I'd sort out the seating after the lesson. I returned to the blackboard.

I tapped on it with my fist, rather harder than I intended. Chalk dust flew everywhere. I declared with an air of desperation

" Can anybody here do this sum . . . ?"

No one put their hands up at first. But then slowly *one* hand was raised. The whole class turned to stare, it was . . .

. . . The hand of the *school inspector* - sat at the back of the classroom.

"Thank you." I muttered weakly. Not sure what to do next, I stared up at the heavens and thought of the old Star Trek line -

"BEAM ME UP SCOTTY!"

Robert Taylor

Mice

Outside the air was sharp
Inside, thick and fetid
Unwashed clothes
Stale food.
rancid
The windows were screwed down
A pathetic attempt to deter vandals
Who came
All the same
Wreaking havoc

The geriatric radiators shuddered
Children lolled languid
Chewing pencils
Yawning
Some wrote
Absorbed
For others, writing was soporific
With no real purpose for their lives
They tried
Without pride
Covering pages.

I sat listening to Simon read
His words catapulted
Through the air
Staccato
Without meaning
'and/the/black/bee/tle/fell
into /the/ stew'
He paused and looked at me
Face wreathed in incredulity
'Poor little sod, his wife went off
 with that red ant
and now he's blinking drowned
in someone's stew
I just can't credit it
Can you?'

Well! Full marks for comprehension
It was the first time the reading scheme
 had meant a thing to me
Simon continued his conversation
'Funny though
When I read that bit you know

When the blue mouse
Was in the shoe house
Well, it was funny
Because there was one'

'One what,' I asked with puzzled air
'A mouse just by your shoe'
My feet were bare
The shoes were there
Lying
And inside one there sat a mouse
Preening his sinister whiskers.
A scream came
I stifled same
Raising my feet...quickly.

A fat grey mouse was chewing my shoe
And another was running towards me
'A mouse, a mouse, there's a blinking mouse
Squealed Gemma as she leapt on her chair
'There's another Miss, over there'
Oooh look, it's tails like leather
'Aaah poor things they're cold in all this weather
Oh aren't they lovely!'
Cooed Tracy 'this ones only a baby
Poor little thing I bet its hungry.'

'We've got loads o them in our house
What a load o fuss about a mouse.'

'Mice,' I said in teacher mode
'The plural of mouse is mice'
But they couldn't hear a word
It really wasn't nice.

Children were chanting rhythmically
Several high-pitched screams
Nodding and beaming
Manic grins
Dancing eyes
Prattling like demented ducks
Jimmy racing
Arms flailing
Chasing mice
Not nice
Help!

We never tackled this at college

But yes... the secret sign
I stood on chair
Raise my hand
They understand
Like a poor relation of the statue of liberty
I stood quite still and waited.
They did the same
I called no name
Quiet... as mice.

With quavering voice I started singing
'A mouse lived in a windmill in old Amsterdam
A windmill with a mouse in and he wasn't grousing'
They sang
Watching mice
For signs of vocal talent.

Trevor smiled beautifically
'I can hear them squeaking
I think they like it'

I dispatched a child to find the head
Before beginning '3 blind mice'
Then 'six little mice sat down to spin'
We sang that one twice
The head arrived incredulous
At 20 scampering mice
'Oh well!' he shouted merrily
Makes a change from nits and lice!

Joyce Worsfold

Quatrain (aabb)

Darting ducks delve deep
Ducklings follow with choirboy cheep
Mother duck skims like a sailing ship
But her beak is hard when used like a whip.

Joyce Worsfold

The Caretaker.

When I was a teacher, we had a caretaker at school called Bert.
Bert did not like dirt.
That is, he didn't like cleaning any of it!
He worked at two speeds.
The faster one was - *very slow.*
If you ever wanted anything doing, like changing a light bulb,
you would be lucky to get it done within a week.
Bert had too many distractions.
The working men's club was just over the road from school
and the bookies was next door but one.
If Bert wasn't in the working man's club - he was in the bookies!
He often smelt of beer and cigarettes.
I believe that the teaching staff did not like him very much
and he didn't speak to most of them if he could avoid it.
When he was in school, he hid away in a broom cupboard and listened to sport
on the radio.
Bert did speak to me though.
For some reason, he always took it upon himself,
To let me know the latest sports results.

He would walk into my classroom with a black rubbish bag,
empty my dustbin and say something like -
'They're 426 for 5.'
And I'd think - Hm, That must be cricket!
And I'd say, 'That's a pretty good score, that isn't it?'
And he'd reply. 'Hardly. Not when the other lot are batting! We've got to bat
next. Dearie me!'
And then he'd leave the room.
The next day he'd walk in saying; 'Tut! Tut! Tut! They're 146 all out! Now
they've got to follow on. Typical of our lot! Hopeless shower!'
And he would leave.
From that, I would gather that the English cricket team were not doing very well.
The next day he'd walk in and say -
'He's just won. Black ball game. What a finish.'
And I'd think....snooker - and I'd wonder who was playing.
The next day it would be.....
'He's just got a hole in one at the short seventeenth.'
And I'd think - Mm, mm – 'Golf!'
Or it would be
'Gold Crest has won by four lengths'
And I'd think – 'horse racing!'
'66 -1 it was an' all !' He added.
'Did you have a bet on it?' I asked.
'Are you kidding.' He replied. 'If I had had ten quid on that thing, do you think
I'd be here now?'
He'd gone before I had a chance to ask the question - 'Where would you have

gone - if you had won? '

The working men's club I guessed - and drink away his winnings. Or put it all on another horse!

One day we were about to break up for Christmas, the children had left and I was sharing a bottle of Beaujolais in my classroom with two of the female teaching staff and we were rather giggly - when the caretaker walked in.

'Fancy some wine Bert?' I asked him.

He looked at the bottle and pulled a face.

'Mm. that's Jollybow, that is. My wife drinks that, but I don't like it myself. Much prefer the beer.'

The two ladies giggled. Not only had he got the name of the wine wrong of course but we all *knew* he drunk beer!

'I've just had some bad news actually, from the doctor.' Bert added. 'He told me that I've got to take things easy from now on.'

More suppressed laughter followed from my two colleagues. The idea of him 'taking things easy' was a bit rich!

Then he added more;

'The doctor said that I've got to work at a much slower pace.'

By now, the two ladies could hardly contain themselves.

But Bert continued.

'He said, that I've got this disease. It's called *Euthanasia.* '

At which point, my two female colleagues, disappeared in to my classroom stock room -trying to choke back their obvious hysterical laughter.

I said; 'Don't mind them Bert. It is Christmas and the end of term. And they've had a few. I'm sorry to hear about your bad news.'

'That's alright.' said Bert, turning and walking away.

He paused at the doorway and added.

'The news from Australia is - they're 246 for 5 - if you're interested.'

'Oh, thanks Bert.' I said, and he left.

The two ladies poured out of the stockroom, laughing fit to burst. The tears of laughter were streaming down their faces.

'He's got *euthanasia!*' they cried. 'Bert's got *euthanasia!*'

Then one of them added.

'Poor Bert! We shouldn't laugh! That's a serious disease. Euthanasia - kills you know!'

At which point, we all laughed at the absurdity at what she had just said. We knew what he had really meant though. He meant *emphysema.*

Tut! Tut! Poor Bert!

Robert Taylor

Unfinished symphony

Lisa had a temper
Lisa banged doors
Lisa hated everyone
Lisa had claws

Everyone moaned about Lisa
She drove everyone spare
Every lesson was boring
Lisa just didn't care

She sang loudly through literacy hour
And chanted obscenities at break
Her prowess at fighting gave power
But in lessons she was hardly awake.

There's Beethoven playing on Radio 3
Mendelssohn, Mussorgsky and Bach
There's a Hockney exhibition that interests me
And in London, Julius Caesar and Joan of Arc.
But none of it matters to Lisa
And probably it never will
Unless someone learns how to please her,
Breaks the spell and allows her talent to spill.

We tried to teach her the recorder
Mixed powder paint and gave her a brush
She punched and she thumped out of order
And gave Marvin and Gavin a push.

Then…
On a cold day in May
They came to play,
A string quintet.

They opened their cases,
tuned up and played.
And I watched the faces
as the music swelled.
Lisa was listening, Lisa enthralled
Lisa was glowing, each instrument called.
Cadences trembled, soaring, sweet
Musette and minuet fell at her feet.
Goosebumps raised on tingling flesh,
violin and viola intermingle and mesh.
The slow low tone, rich and mellow,
Lisa is longing to draw bow on cello.

'A whole class of kids learn the violin?
Can you imagine the chaos and din?
Kids like this just need to count and to read
You'll be wasting your time, like teaching the creed.'

'But what if there's a Kennedy or Menuhin
Lurking in year four or five?
What if there's a foetus growing that will never come alive?'

'They can sing, can't they, play the recorder and hum
There's a limit to what can be done on the National Curriculum'

Nevertheless, we got what we needed...eventually...
Cases lay open, violins gleaming like chestnuts in shells.
Children were hushed as they waited for their music to swell.
They learned the correct stance
and made their bows dance,
fingers placed firmly on strings.
they learned which was which
And just how to switch
between notes and then their music had wings.
And Lisa?
Well she had the cello
She sat and she hugged it tight
and learned to make music not bellow
and her eyes when she played were so bright.
She wrote a poem about it later
It didn't rhyme or scan, have alliterations or simile
It simply said,

*'The cello is cool, it makes a sad sound
And the person who's playing is me.'*

Joyce Worsfold

69

Oh dear! what can the matter be?

Oh dear, what can the matter be,
The head went out and absentmindedly,
locked the staff room door, with his own key
and the teaching staff, are in there.

The head's gone to the bank, with a bag full of money.
He locked the wrong door and the staff, think it's funny.
They've laughed 'til they cried, now their tears are all runny
and no one knows they're locked in.

It isn't the only thing, the head has forgotten.
There was the Monday staff meeting
which the staff, think is rotten.
Now they're saying three cheers to their head Mr. Cotton.
Now they're ever so glad they're locked in.

Now it's well after one, there's a knock on the door.
They should have been teaching, fifteen minutes before.
They slip a wee note, straight under the door.
Saying, 'Help! We're all locked in here!'

The children who find it, work out what to do,
They can't help but giggle, but the teachers do too.
Except Mrs. Clark, who is needing the loo.
But at least someone knows they're in there.

The caretaker's arriving, with a spare key.
He's swearing and cursing, as he lets them all free.
They've disturbed him, while he was watching T.V.
The first test has started today!

The children are happy, they've been longer at play.
The staff, have been happy, while the head's been away.
And the cancelled staff meeting, is a bonus they say!
And a dinner time with three cups of tea. Ole!!

Robert Taylor

Embroidery

Embroider me, but better than I am
For a woman's shortcomings
Clamber out of cupboards,
call in cobwebs and
bellow in the dust.

My failings are spread on floors for all to see
Like winged beasts
But even then it's fiction woven in tapestry.

Stitch me strands on which to stand
for I am needle-sharp,
A roaring lioness who dares
to travel further.
And my needle is threaded,
ready to weave my silken threads
and break the chains.

Joyce Worsfold

A Blind God?

Your tongue stubs toes,
Pricks fingers,
blocks veins.
It squeezes and crushes.
You are
A firelighter
Earth trampler
Scandal seeker
Warmonger.
And yet...He loves YOU.

Joyce Worsfold

A Multicultural Education

The man came
To put his child's name
On the waiting list
A tall, stately Kenyan
Who moved with dignity.
'Child's name?' I asked
poised with pen
'Moreblessings he replied and then
'Moreblessings, smiling bright
'Moreblessings?' I asked wondering
If I had heard aright.
He gave me an enormous grin
He had eyes that love lived in
'Five little girls, God gave to me
But I longed for one son
With such intensity.
But as you see, another daughter
And as I kneeled before the altar
God laughed uproariously
And said' More blessings'
Yes, six little girls he gave to me!

From Pakistan came Shabana and Shameem
Thick glossy plaits
And glowing, excited eyes
Tomorrow is Eid Miss and we'll get a surprise
New clothes and parties
Like your Christmas holiday
Their words tumbled over there was so much to say
When we come back we'll bring a party for you too
And all the children will share it
Because that's what we do!
And they did.

'Good Morning Head Teacher!' saluted Su Ying
The only words in English he knew to bring
But he worked so hard, with such vigorous intensity
And six weeks later could talk the hind legs off a donkey
One day he came to me, irate and seething.
'That boy was rude to me, he swears and say I am thick
I would like you to hit him with a big stick.'
I explained that violence only makes things worse.
'Not in Taiwan' he started to curse
Later we talked, the swearing boy, him and me
We shared a few laughs and a very English cup of tea.

Then they played football and Su Ying scored
Wayne hugged him and cheered
Su Ying said it wasn't as bad as he feared.

Meinbowla came from Malawi
With the biggest smile I ever saw
He'd never been in a school before
In Africa he'd been taught by his mother
His village had no school and no teacher.
'Are you nervous, Meinbowla?' I asked
'A little but I think that by this days end
I might even have a friend!'
He was so naive, unspoilt and good
I feared that he would be misunderstood
At the end of the day
I made my way
To the classroom
Full of foreboding
Worry and gloom.
But found a bubbling happy place
He ran towards me,
 excitement written across his face
'When the teacher asked who would like to be a friend of mine
They all put up their hands
So now I have twenty nine.'

Jennifer was a black South African
Her Mum had suffered torture and pain
She dreamed of her homeland
But knew she could never go there again
Jennifer was quiet, timid and withdrawn
Who worried about bullying, name calling and scorn
But there came a day when Jenny danced into school
Beaming and bouncing and bright
'Have you heard about *my* Mr Mandela… he is free
I saw him on the television last night
And Jennifer grew in stature
And IJennifer held her head proud
And told everyone of Mr. Mandela
Confident, clear and loud.

Yugoslavia appeared to be a seething mass of hate
Another war where vengeance could never come too late
Marcus was a Bosnian Serb
And for months he had not heard
From his grandparents living there
He was full of fear and care
At Christmas he bought me a crystal heart

73

'Miss, its to show people should not live apart
No one can love enough'
He placed it proudly on my window sill
I loved it then, I have it still.
Bina came from Iraq when six years old
And now our countries were at war
When she heard that my son in law
Was a soldier sent to fight
She wrote for me a precious letter
Just to make me feel the better
'I do hope that you son law is all right
I would not like you to be sad
Because I know the truth
That war is very bad.'
Many more children from many other places
All waiting in assembly with expectant upturned faces
I tried to teach them right from wrong
I tried to help them to be strong
I tried to show them loving care
But I learned from them so much more
than I had ever learned before.

Joyce Worsfold

No feelings.

I'd like to touch her hand and feel vibrations down my spine.
I'd like to be tender to her, just once in a while,
Dash my head against a tree, like Heathcliffe did,
calling; 'Cathy! Cathy!'

But you see it's just no good.
I've got no feelings,
what are feelings?
I don't feel feelings,
the way that I should.

They bare their souls out on T.V.
And in the movies,
And I'm not sure.
Is that how others feel, or are supposed to?
Or is it just for show?
I only wish that I could see, what others see,
Is there anyone here like me, with emptiness inside?

I've got no feelings,
what are feelings?
I don't feel feelings,
I've been denied.

As I sit and glance through the papers,
What should I feel about the starving?
some kind of pity?
some kind of horror?
What I don't feel is quite alarming.

And when my best friend died, did I cry?
No I kept it all concealed.
Bottled up inside, like cut glass in my chest.
Nothing was revealed.
There was a kind of dull ache inside.
I only wish that I had cried.
I wished I could have cried!

I had some feelings,
some sort of feelings,
but I kept my feelings,
deep inside.

Robert Taylor

A Funny name for God!

Dear Lord, our father, what's the proper way of praying?
Do I kneel like this? Or do I sit cross legged?

When praying, I always put my hands flat together like this.
Brian Makey in our class, says that they are called palms.
But they can't be.
Palms are those little poems that you wrote in the Bible God.

When praying, I always put the fingers of each hand flat together.
Even the thumbs go together.
That's proper praying that is.
I never bend my fingers, or fasten them together.
And I always keep my eyes tightly closed when praying.
I never peep.
Some do at school. I've seen them!
But I never do!

'Our Father Whichart in heaven....'
Whichart? Father Whichart?
In heaven ?
It's a funny name for God that.
Fancy God being called Father Whichart?
Imagine?
Father Whichart!
It's a funny name for God that!

'Our Father Whichart in heaven -
Harold be thy name.'
Harold! Harold!
Harold be thy name?
That's a funny name for God too.
Fancy God being called Harold.
Imagine!
Father.....Harold....Whichart -
Fancy God being called that!

It's funny, but I've never heard God called those names before.
Not in any other place but this one.
But they must be God's names
because this is *his* prayer.
It's called 'The Lord's Prayer.'
So, it must be true.
Father.....Harold....Whichart.
Imagine!
But then, you've got lots of names haven't you God.
There is - our father,

76

And God,
And the Lord God,
And the Lord God Almighty,
And the Holy Spirit,
And the Holy Ghost,
And then there is Father Whichart -
And Harold!
(As mentioned in this poem!)

Why do you need all those names?
I suppose you need them...
so that.....so that.....so that....
I've got it!.....it's so that you can be in all
those different places in the world -
all at the same time.
Watching over me in England,
saying my prayers at night,
in the winter time.
While watching over others in - Australia -
Saying their prayers in *our* daytime -
But in their Summer time.

And then you've got to be home in heaven,
watching over all those dead people too.
Like Romans......and Vikings.....
And dinosaurs....
And my pet hamster - Derek.
And my granddad - Jack.
Not to mention your own son, Jesus.
You know, I'm sorry he died, God -
Because if he hadn't, God,
You'd be a *granddad* by now!

But how do you listen to them all at once?
I suppose you must have ears like Sky Transmitters!
(And ever so many pairs of 'em!)
And how do you watch over them all?
I expect, you've got a really strong pair of binoculars.
And eyes in the back of your head,
Which my mum says she could do with -
to look after my sisters and me.
Amen.

Robert Taylor

Thunder-cloud

What hope for you my coal-eyed king?
In crowded class-room that threatens oblivion.
A cumulative hatred,
A lightning streak
Zig-zagging all your sagging years.

Your mother anaesthetised by nine births
To all those fathers of forgotten features
and none from which to pull a cord.
What hope?
When penitence is unheard of
Stone blank on your face, solidified.
What hope?

I watched you when the clown tumbled into school,
Infant faces were mobilised by joy.
Laughter exploded and rolled from cheek to cheek.
Rounded eyes shot fire and light,
but yours remained lace-curtained.

Your quick-fire intellect,
Un-kindled by council shacks,
gagged by giro.
What hope?

I read it in the paper, my coal-eyed king
A loveless cell, a rope
A hanging thing.

Joyce Worsfold

The Outing.

I saw you yesterday
All six of you
Shambling in, holding hands
Two of you clinging
Like broken saplings
It took some time to seat you
around the table.
Steel chairs with vinyl seats
Grabbed at you,
You were so afraid and
leapt up and up
howling consternation.
Those around tut-tutted,
shook heads
averted eyes.
I practiced a smile and you seized on at it
Chortling and pointing
It disappeared.
Six pairs of eyes
broken mirrors of nonsense.
One of you broke away
Monkey arms flailing
and bayed at your reflection
in stainless-steel fittings.
Neon-lit signs terrified
"Sausage chips and peas"
are devil whips and darkened dreams.
You cover your head and curl
a wounded hedgehog
on a cafeteria floor.

They lift you, one each side
And frog-march to a van
And I see you rocking
 back and forth
and all around, teacups

Joyce Worsfold

Cold Comfort

An un-curtained window
A bare plaster wall
A narrow bed
Where the shadows fall.
Stiff with urine, unwashed sheets
With arms spread wide, one child sleeps
Thumb in mouth the other weeps
Cold is the night
Locked is the door

Home alone kids
Not knowing more.

The huddled one sighs and whispers a fight
'I'll do you, our Dean, if you wet t' bed tonight'

At school the next morning situation is dire
The boiler is broken, a faulty wire
Ice slakes the windows
Wind tunnels through
The water is frozen
Staff say, 'No can do'

Out in the playground
All muffled up
Warming my hands on a coffee cup

To parents we try to give explanation
But we are met with consternation
'Take him home, no way
I'm Christmas shopping today!'

'You're not palming the kids off on us
I can't understand all the fuss'

'No, our house is cold
Electrics cut off'

'She'll be better off 'ere
Me bairn's got a cough'

Some take them home
Others are deaf to our pleas
Convinced that the staff crave a life of ease.
Suddenly my eye is caught,

by Jamie, thin and frail
Walking stiffly down the path
His face unearthly pale
He sways and I catch him
Just before he falls
A bag of frozen bones
Wide-eyed children call

'Eh, did you see that then
Jamie's copped it'
'He's been real bad
since his mother hopped it'

'I reckon it's rabies bet he's been bitten'
'Yeh, he's got a great bulldog
I've only a kitten.'

'No... he's been shot
I saw the sniper'

'No it were a snake bite
a python or viper'

'Don't be daft, he's just got the flu'
'No, it were a dagger..and 'eres one for you'

'I bet it's Aids; he's been sleeping around
He's slept at Darren's and at Ben's he were found'

Where's this imagination when they are writing?
'Come on class 4 and stop that fighting.'

They're shepherded into the classroom
Like worried sheep
While fraught frozen teachers
Try order try to keep.

Jamie is left in very good hands
I rack my brains and try to understand.

We do a lot of P.E. ... fully clothed
We sing and we clap
And our faces glow.
Because we wear gloves we do oral maths
We double up in classes
And wish more had baths.
And over it all, the ambulance siren whines
So they run to the window

And twitter and sign.

'Well, he can't be dead else it'd be a hearse'
'But, he looked really bad, he could 'ave got worse'

Saved by the bell
Playtime at last
And I rush to the staff-room
As the vehicle careers past.

The staff room is eerie
We are all filled with dread
We wait stomachs churning
Then in comes the head

Jamie will live
But we'll all bear the scars
No child of our time should fight such wars
Risen from a wet bed
Having slept in his clothes
He walked to school without breakfast
And quite simply.....froze.

Joyce Worsfold

What goes on in a dog's head?

What goes on in a dog's head?
Well, in this dogs head,
 There are several different walks, by the river, through the woods,
Across the fields, over the moor, by the waterfall, and along the lane to the pub.
(His master's favourite!)

In this dog's head,
There is a favourite tin of dog food, a chew, a special crunchy dog biscuit,
and some exceptionally smelly and chewy dried tripe.
Plus - anything which happens to fall from a human's food table.
(Cakes, buns, crisps and bacon sandwiches are his favourite!)

In this dog's head,
There is a comfortable settee,
A sheepskin rug by the fire,
a quiet spot in the back porch.
And best of all, a spot in front of his master's feet (wherever they are – he is!).

In this dog's head,
There are several dogs he likes.
A sheepdog, a couple of retrievers, a mongrel,
(Who vaguely looks like him – but only vaguely)
And there is a Labrador he secretly loves.
(But un-secretly, pines for!)
There are a couple of terriers he despises, and a Rottweiler he hates!

This dog has a quiet spot in the garden.
There is a hot spot, and a shady spot,
And a spot behind the shed where he can admire the bitch from next door.
And there is another secret spot,
Which only he knows about.
(well, so he thinks anyway!)

In this dog's head,
There is a night class for humans,
Where he would take his master and his mistress.
In this night class,
The dogs would teach the humans how to –
Sit and *stay, and beg and roll over*
And *wag their imaginary tails.*
Now that would be some test to take!
The dog smiles at such a thought.
(He smiles by wagging his tail – of course!)

Robert Taylor

83

Fish and Chips.

Mum was looking in the cupboard, thinking;

'What can I give them all for tea?'
She looked at t' packets, she looked at tins
And then she looked at me and said ;
'Do you want Bolognaise? Or chilli ? Or curry?
You know, something exotic I can cook in a hurry?'
Well, our Kate reminded her,
That hot stuff gave her t' runs,
So mum said;
'In that case, will you settle for burgers in buns?'
Well, we didn't fancy that
or sausages and mash.
Or fish fingers and beans.
We weren't that adventurous.

Mum said; 'You are finicky and very hard to please.
So, tell me then, the three of you, what do you want for your teas?'
Well we didn't even hesitate, Phil, Kate and I,
We spoke up as one voice.
'Fish and chips!' was our reply.

'Fish and chips, fish and chips,
It's fish and chips for me.
Fish and chips, fish and chips,
give us them for tea. Please!'

One day, dad came home looking all elated,
He said;
'Our luck has changed. I must say it's belated.
Wash your hands and face, and put on your best togs.
We're off out celebrating, because I've just won on
t' dogs.
We're going out for a meal, not to a snack bar,
or a caff,
we're going to a posh restaurant. It's expensive so don't laugh.'

It were posh an' all, I tell you, with carpets hung on't walls.
And dishes to wash your hands in, and serviettes and all!
And when the waiter, (done up like a penguin)
Handed over t' menu.
Dad gasped ; 'It's all in French. Francaise? Parlez Vous?'
And our Kate, who'd had lessons in French,
More than twice at school,
tried to decipher't menu.

She said ; 'I can do it as a rule.
This pommes thing, means potatoes.
And this bit means frogs legs.
I'm told they're quite delicious,
but I'll have something else instead.'
Auntie Claire asked for; 'Sirloin steak.'
And Uncle Ted asked for; 'Duck!'
And our Kate, who thinks that she's all grown up,
asked for some foreign muck.
She said; 'Veal Parmigiana, please.'

Me mum was undecided, but liked the sound of 42.
'42. An omelette with a sort of salad - tossed.'
While dad, who was wishing his dog had lost,
really hadn't a clue.
He just stared mystified at menu.
'If Pommes is potatoes - what is chips?'
Then it came to our turn to order
And this sound echoed from our lips.
'We don't care what it says on't menu,
Just give us fish and chips.

Fish and chips, fish and chips,
It's fish and chips for me.
Fish and chips, fish and chips,
give us them for tea. Please!'

Then dad at last decided.
'Hi! Fish and chips will do.'
And mum and Claire and Uncle Ted,
Changed their minds and had them too.
Even Kate had second thoughts,
She said; 'Hee! I don't like to confuse t' waiter.
So, I'll have fish and chips as well.
I can have a fancy dish later.'

But the waiter went all ashen faced,
And he did not look too pleased.
When dad said;
'Waiter! Make that fish and chips all round?
And have you any - mushy peas?'

So, it was.......
'Fish and chips, fish and chips,
It's fish and chips for me.
Fish and chips, fish and chips,
give us them for tea.
Please!'

Robert Taylor

Growing Up

She endures the miracle of birth.
Her midwife smacks her.
She cries.
She goes to school.
She misbehaves.
Her teacher punishes her.
She cries.
She becomes aware of her body.
She notices its changing condition.
She wears her first bra.
She cries.
She swots for exams.
She takes exams.
She fails exams.
She cries.
She starts work.
She finds it deadly boring.
She meets a boy.
They fall in love.
They get married.
Her mother cries!

Robert Taylor

Ice-Cream Parlour

The prattle of tea-cups
The hush-swish-hush of coffee machine
Purple light and plastic chairs in underwater green.
What shall I choose?
A large knickerbocker,
Cappachino or mocha?
A children's Diddy-cup, Fizzy-float
A warm Belgian waffle or a jelly-boat?

I limber up my tongue
And view the plastic dome.
Lemon cheesecake, scone or spiced curd tart.
When on earth will I ever start?
Hot chocolate with whipped cream choc-flake or mallow
Expectant faces drool and swallow.
Wide-eyed mopple-tots are strident in their choosing
Soft-haired senior citizens are quieter in their musing.
I spy, ice-cream
Honeycomb, toffee and blueberry pie
Blackcurrant, rhubarb and strawberry, sigh!
Service,
Silence
Eat slowly, Stop and savour
Taste-buds tingle
Every flavour.
Look around, lick lips, such gratification
Mellow music, sighs, buzz of conversation.

A psychedelic cyclist sips
A lemon leaf tea with herbal hips.
Weary walkers rest and imbibe
Hot soup simmered, soothing inside

But ice-cream is queen
Over all the rest
Everyone knows
That ice-cream is best.
Eat slowly,
Sensuously
Flavours sing
Glacial gladness
Textures ring
Lips sliding over silky-iced joy
Frosted pleasure that can never cloy.

Joyce Worsfold

Ice-cold in a coffee-shop

Laughing we entered, flushed with the success of gifts well chosen,
'A table for two, non-smoker'
A quiet corner
and long awaited sustenance.
Here the happy prattle of tea-cups,
caverns of chocolate-cake, clouds of meringue.
I order scones and double-cream and jam.
The scent of coffee lingers in the air,
Contentment,
a wriggling of toes in man-made soles with leather uppers.
Calloused hands clasp cups
and tight lips loosen.

In that glorious place,
Halfway between lips and cream,
She tugs a reluctant corner of my eye
dragging it screaming from cream, to ashes.
Sadness hangs dripping
on her waxen face.
And, inevitable as hunger
pain has etched its cruel scrawl.
She is empty-eyed, veiled in freezing fog
She stirs her tea disconsolately
Round and round and round and round.

He sits opposite, eagerly leaning towards her, the chrysalis of his love?
A friendly, hot-water-bottle-man
enveloped in Arran, hand-knitted.
He attempts fruitless conversation,
a duvet of sound,
gentling her with hot-chocolate eyes.
She remains still,
like a whale imprisoned in Arctic ice,
racked beneath interminable snow.
Outside the rain scythes through Christmas curtained streets
And a crisp 'Silent Night' flutes faultless in air.
But out there
the alien city is unmanageable dark
Here she is masked, fast-frozen until someone can melt
a channel past predatory pain

Joyce Worsfold

That's all we need!

Mum, dad, Phil Kate and me
have just been abroad.
(That's where you go over t' sea).
We went to Manchester
and hopped on a plane
and three hours later
we were on t' beach in Spain.
Well, it wasn't like that actually.
It never is with us.
Nothing is ever plain sailing.
(Or should I say, *plane flying?)*
There's always a lot of fuss.

It was the night before in t' front lounge.
You should have seen our faces,
When our mum staggered in t' front room,
with her clothes in *three* full cases.
'There you are! That's me packed!'
She said.
'There are regulations about luggage!'
roared dad. 'You're out of your tiny mind.
If we have to take all three cases,
then I suggest we leave you behind!'

We managed to persuade her,
That planes were not like boats.
There has to be less room for luggage,
so that you can squeeze in all o' t' folks.
Plane 'ud never get off o' t' runway.
It 'ud be like Wright Brothers first flight.
'We're ten foot off the ground Captain,
but already losing height!'

All mum could say was,
'I squeezed in everything really tight.'
So dad, opened all her cases
and it was soon revealed-
six woolly jumpers, four blankets,
One corsette and a shopping bag on wheels!
'What's this for?' boomed dad.
'That's just in case they have supermarkets in Spain!' Mum said.
We all laughed.
'Well, they might have!' she added.
Next we saw some things,
we never knew she possessed.

A pair of woolly knickers,
which stretched, from knees to chest.
Mum said ; 'These are thermal. I never go without.
They stop you getting cold in places *you* don't even know about.'
Then me dad, did his religious bit.
He said words we're not supposed to say.
And when our Phil, repeated 'em,
He got clouted straight away.
'Where we're going, Gladys.' said dad,
'It'll be extremely hot.
You'll not need thermal underware.
Or any clothes like as not.'

And our Kate said;
'You'll not get me going topless.'
And dad, who is no diplomat, said; 'Kid!
Since you look much the same either way round,
It wouldn't matter much if you did!'

Then Kate stormed off to her room.
'I'm going to bed. And I don't think I even want to go tomorrow.'
And mum and dad disagreed.
And mum ended up sobbing and said;
'Ooh! That's all we need!'

Next day, we were good and ready,
Except for t' last minute rush -
checking for gas, closing windows, cancelling milk and stuff.
Finding passports and tickets,
and checking for air in t' tyres,
and mum dashing back into the house,
At last minute, just to make sure she'd turned off all of t' fires!

So, at last, we were on our way,
Each listing the things we might have forgotten.
And when mum said;
'Whoa! What about camera?'
Dad took on someat rotten.
'Gladys! That was not my territory.
Not my thing to pack.
Anyway, if *you've* forgotten it,
It's too late to go back!'

Well, we made it to the airport on time.
With five minutes left to spare.
But with my dad complaining that he'd sprouted a few more grey bits in his hair.

Then we actually got on the plane on time.

And we heard the engines - roar!
Well, one of 'em roared to be precise,
But there should have been - *one more.*
It took nearly an hour to get that engine to start,
And dad joked;
'Hee! It'ud be quicker by horse and cart!'
Then the captain over t' intercom,
laid it on the line.

He said; 'The engines are now working,
That's the good news.....
But the bad news is, we've missed our take off time.
And I'm afraid, that the next available slot is in .....*three hours time!'*

Then our Phil added to t' despair.
He said; 'Me nose has started to bleed.'
And mum got all angry and annoyed and said;
'Ooh! That's all we need!'

An hour out over t' sea, we ran into bad weather,
plane lurched back and forward
and threw us all together.
And there were thundering, and there were lightning,
And t' plane plunged thousands of feet,
And mum as she was sick in her paper bag,
Gasped; 'Urgh! That's all we need!'

And when we landed in Spain,
We got a dreadful shock.
They couldn't find our luggage,
They'd lost the blooming lot.
And it wouldn't stop raining,
It was just like being home in Leeds.
With me mum, crossing her arms and complaining;
'Oooh! That's all we need!'

Well, it couldn't last, we hoped.
And soon, out came the sun.
So, we went out onto the terrace,
to get ourselves well done.
But our Kate over did it
and instead of a tan, to impress all t' blokes,
She went all red and blotchy
And got herself sunstroke.
Then Phil, the glutton, as we call him
because he stuffs himself through greed,
He got that there Spanish tummy.
And mum hissed; 'That's all we need!'

Mum stayed in the shade most of the time,
While dad ogled the girls round the pool,
until he slipped and fell in fully clothed.
Hee! He didn 't half feel a fool!
One day, we sat round t' swimming pool,
writing postcards home.
usual stuff like – 'Nice grub here!'
And - 'There was a lizard in my room!'
Phil was still suffering with Spanish tummy.
While sunburn drove Kate spare.
So, when we wrote – 'Wish you were here!'
They wrote – 'Wish we were there!'

When we'd finished writing t' postcards,
They were caught by a sudden breeze.
And as we watched them blow into
t' swimming pool,
Mum spluttered; 'Ooh! That's all we need!'

But when they asked us afterwards;
'Well, did you enjoy yourselves in Spain?'
We cheered and said unanimously;
'Yeah, great! Can we go there again!'

Then a smile played across dad's lips
and he looked kind of pleased.
He turned to mum and they said together.

'Ah! That's all we need!'

Robert Taylor

The Whitby Triangle.

There was Gladys, Mabel, me and Joe,
our kids, their kids and t' dog in tow.
In t' Morris minor and their old van,
out for the day on Whitby sands.
While t' wives played bingo
And t' kids machines
and stuffed 'emselves with hot dogs and ice creams.
Joe and me, fancied some quiet and peace,
So we hired a rowing boat, it costs   10 quid each.

Joe said he knew all about boats and sea.
He'd seen boat race last year on T.V.
Hee! I was glad he was at my side
because he knew all about currents and tide.
(Daft happorth lied!)

What gave me an eerie feeling,
what made my nerve ends jangle,
what sent my senses reeling,
could it be?.....Oh, could it be?
That there's a 'Whitby Triangle?'

Three hours later, Gladys wore a frown.
She said; 'Time enough, for blighters to have drowned!'
But what had her fretting and caused a to do,
Was my cheque book was missing and me car keys too!
(Silly Moo!)

She called for t' coastguard, told them all she knew.
'They're hopeless in a crisis and a rotten crew!'
Well, lifeboat was launched and raced out to sea,
and it vanished in't mist for what seemed an eternity.

Three hours later, there was panic in the air.
They called for an helicopter.
'We'll find them if they're there!'
It flew round t' abbey and out over t' bay,
And our Darren said; 'It's been a smashing day!'

But what gave them an eerie feeling,
what made their nerve ends jangle,
what sent their senses reeling,
could it be?....Oh, could it be?
That there's a 'Whitby Triangle?'
The 'copter wasn't back, after an hour or two,
so the coastguard hitched a lift, from a trawler crew.

'If I'm more than an hour, I'll tell thee what to do,
Send for t' Royal Navy, they'll send a ship or two.'

Somewhere through the mist, he heard the sound of bells ringing,
then he realised, that it were men folk singing.
It was the lifeboat men, the 'copter crew,
Joe and me,
On this great licensed oil rig, in the middle o' North Sea.
(Hi ! And it was duty free!)

Joe called out;
'You're too late to disappear.
There are plenty of spirits, but we've drunk all t' beer!'
Such a paradise was that three legged frame,
A free house, with real ale,
Whitby Triangle was its name.

But what gave us an eerie feeling,
what made our nerve ends jangle,
what sent our senses reeling,
was that t' brewery had never heard of –
'The Whitby Triangle..

Robert Taylor with Mike Hone

When Arthur came to our school.

Before I performed my poetry and stories at a school in North Yorkshire,
I was asked by one teacher, if I was the same person who had visited her son's
school a few weeks earlier. She told me the name of the school and I confessed
that it was me. This was a conversation she told me she had had with her son
after my visit
BOY: We had someone reading poems in our school today.
MUM: Oh, what was his name?
BOY: Oh, I don't know. Arthur - somebody or other.
MUM: Arthur? Oh!
The next day, as she dropped her child off at school, the lady asked her child's
teacher, who Arthur was . . .
The teacher was nonplussed at first;
"Arthur! No, it doesn't ring any bells! Hang on! (Then she giggled) We did have
an *author* in school though!

Robert Taylor

Body Beautiful

The voice was disembodied
yet sounds normally
considering from where it came.
A flame eaten body,
in a hospital ward,
an intimate friend of pain.
She calls and her voice is like a sword,
That pierces feckless folk like me.
I shrink back,
a soul without it's packaging
is too much to contemplate.
We talk of souls,
but do not begin to understand
what comprises love... or hate.
Do we even begin to worship God?
Do we worship the body?
Is that the path we've always trod?
Let's face it
Finely chiselled profiles influence our lives.
The line of breast, the sway of hips,
Glossy hair, caught shining in the sun
The rosy sheen of smiling lips
The battle with cosmetics, fought and won.

Where is the voice of God for me,
can it ever be on page three?
She asks for a kiss
It could kindle no desire.
Her body would struggle to light
any hidden fire.

Yet...she gives love
Craves love
Is love
When then is ugliness a bar to joy?
What really unlocks love,
uncorks love,
enfolds love?
Is our love really so shallow?
Must the love of bodies destroyed
lie for ever fallow?

He...
Is a soul disembodied,
a voice crying out in the dark.
His body scathed and whipped and nailed

and hung to rot on bark.
Darkness, blood and burning pain,
Yet this soul rose and will rise again.

Come Christ, in the darkness of my life.
strip aside the hypocrisy of my shell,
enter every private hell
and join with every lonely soul
to make every naked spirit whole.

Joyce Worsfold

Concentration

After thirteen days of longing
They let me see her.
I put my lips to the glass.
Cold glass.
We kiss but cannot touch.
My arms ache empty.
Cold arms
Numb brain
Tearing pain.
I tremble with fear for her,
child of my womb.
To me, who should be stronger,
She communicates strength.
She who once screamed at spiders.
She who shrieked whenever I left her side.
She smiles and softly says
"I shall adjust"
The guards,
Cold eyes
Cold hearts
Curled lips
Sneer.
Anger flares in me.
Threatens to envelop me.
Blinds so I cannot see,
But she sees,
Presses her lips to the glass
The cold glass mists with the heat of her faith,
I warm my cheek against it
'Mummy, we must not hate...'

Joyce Worsfold

A mother's anguished blues!

I got that call the other day, the one every mother dreads.
I got that call the other day, the one every mother dreads.
My son will not be coming home and I can't get him out of my head.

From sunrise to sunset, I see his face, all through the day,
From sunrise to sunset I see his face, all through the day,
His face, when he was a little boy – that face will not go away.

I never wanted him to be a soldier. I pleaded with him 'No! No! No!'
I never wanted him to be a soldier. I pleaded with him 'No! No! No!'
But he said; 'It's something I want to do mum, I've got to Go! Go! Go!'

Before they sent him overseas, he looked so smart in his uniform
Before they sent him overseas he looked a darling in his uniform
But as he walked out of the front door, I dreaded that he would not come home!

They say he was a hero; A hero to make one feel proud.
They say he was a hero; A hero to make me feel proud.
But all I feel is this anguish, it make me want to cry out loud!

'Not by baby! No my son!
Not my baby! Not my only one!'

He was doing what he wanted to do. He wanted to go and fight.
He was doing what he wanted to do. He felt that the cause was right.
I wish I shared that ideal. I wish I understood.
But . . .

From sunrise to sunset, I see his face all through the day,
His face, when he was a little boy – that face will not go away.

Robert Taylor

The Road to Mother Care

Suburban English couple
In neat suburban home,
with fridge and flat-screen tele
holidays in Greece and Rome
Suddenly find their life is to become complete
as they await the gentle patter of little tiny feet.
They trudge from Boots to Mothercare
And amass a mass of needs
Baby-cots and bouncers
Steriliser for the feeds.
And Mum to be eats sensibly
Sacrifices wine and cigarettes.
And Dad he paints the nursery,
hangs mobiles and decorettes.
They exercise together
as is the modern trend.
He times breathing and contractions,
finds things for Amazon to send.
There are tests and scans and vitamins
and the birthing pool is booked.
They read a pile of magazines
on babies they are hooked.
At last the joyous moment comes
and relatives gather round
cuddle and coo and he goes home,
happy, healthy and sound.

Worried African couple
In shabby, tin hut shack
With blanket bed and cooking ring
and some meal in a plastic sack
Find that they are to feed one more,
stare out at the stars from their own front door
They hold hands, dream dreams
of a home with food and plenty
Where there are no hungry screams
From bellies aching empty.
The mother continues working
In hot sun in the fields
And father tries to hide his fears
When the harvest fails to yield.
They share their meagre rations
And hold each other, tight
Her belly grows and thickens
throbs between them in the night.
They ache and long for this first-born one,

for a thriving youngster, a beloved son.
At last the joyous moment comes
And she holds him to her breast.
Her man covers her with kisses
and bids her take her rest.
Then he reverently holds his little one
and gently strokes his head.
His tears baptise his beloved son,
Born poor...born dead.

Joyce Worsfold

Children of Africa

You dance on dusty pavements
At night you feel the cold
But you live as sons of shining,
Your smiles are six years old.
Your hearts are many miles wider
Than many hearts will be
And your mother's love for you
Is wondrous, warm and free.
Innocence envelops you
From woolly curls to feet
and our hearts cry out for you
Though we may never meet.

But other hearts have other thoughts
And other hearts are cold
Other hearts see only black
Where we see only gold.
Other hands would crush you
And even stifle life.
Other hands would muffle
Every song you have to sing
For in every trembling feather
They see an eagle's wing.

Your dancing feet, trace patterns
Upon the sands of time
As hand in hand you stand there
Like sons of me and mine.
We feel we are your brothers, your mothers, sisters, friends
and ties will just grow stronger
because real love never ends

Joyce Worsfold

Tanks for Tea

What's for tea, Mum?
Can I have some dumplings and a plate of stew,
And while I'm waiting a crust to chew,
Or beans on toast or even jam and bread?
Come on, Mum,
I'm starving
I feel half dead.

'What's this Mum, on my plate?
Bullets and bombs
Eh, you are in a state.
What do you mean, eat up and grow fat
No-one can survive on that!
I can't eat bombs and Trident submarines,
What's wrong with toasted teacakes, strawberries and cream?
What do you mean, they're radio-active
and the cupboards standing bare,
there's tanks instead of taties
a glut of weapons everywhere.
I'm hungry, Mum, I've an empty tum
My belly needs food not guns.
Go tell 'em down at government
that bombs give me the runs.
None of us kids will ever grow
If all they do is play at war.

Mum what's happened to love and care?
Isn't there any anywhere?
Come on , Mum, what is for tea
Why don't they listen?
Why can't they see?

Joyce Worsfold

Barney and Sam

Barney and Sam
Capricious creatures
Enormous heads and innocent features.
Escalating ears that hold no tune,
Ludicrous cries which very soon
Will tear the peace with blatant clamour,
Long wailing howl, staccato hammer.
Barney and Sam.

Staunch allies, canny collaborators
Errant detectives, skilled investigators,
Who seize the opportune open gate
And never ever stop to wait.
Race a derby down the lane
And me calling and calling over again
Barney and Sam.

Morning birdsong, cockerel cry
Crooked backed beasts would like to fly!
Erupt from stable at a run
Resplendent in the morning sun.
Eager for freedom and flying air
Childlike donkeys, exuberant pair.
Sam nudges me with playful nose,
Then kicks back his legs and goes
Down on the ground and round he rolls.
Dizzy delight in dusty holes
Legs clumsily pedalling air.
I lean on gate and stand and stare
I cannot let the moment pass
Yet some say, the donkey is… an ass

Joyce Worsfold

Oldies

Retriever a heap of golden hair
Reclines on a rug, relaxed and calm
Old man dozes on his high seat chair.
No need for clocks or morning alarm.

Joyce Worsfold

Please do it yourself!
(and then do it for me!)

I'm not much at D. I. Y.
My shelves are a disaster.
Though it takes me hours to put them up,
they come down a darn sight faster!

My very last shelf that fell down,
But that was not my fault.
I only intended it for lighter things,
Like the pepper and the salt.

But my wife, she put on heavy things -
a set of cast iron pans.
I tell you, when they hit the ground.
It was like a jet plane coming into land!

The shelf followed close behind,
To the ground they clattered
And folks came from far and wide
To complain that their peace had been shattered!

I once bought a set of shelf assembly drawers,
the sort with guaranteed success.
You follow their instructions carefully
and hey presto! You make a mess.

I took the pieces out of the box
but as far as I could see,
They'd sent far too many A's.
Only two C's and not a B!

But I hammered the pieces together
and I stuck them all up with glue.
Of course I stuck my fingers up,
But then you do, don't you?

I tried to follow *their* diagrams
but I could not make head nor tail.
So I resolved to do it my way.
I don't know why I failed!

I couldn't open the top drawer
and the whole thing sloped one way.
My wife christened it, 'his disaster unit!'
It's been one - until this day,

Both looking distinctly fragile
And wobbling like a jelly,
if you should just but touch it.
It weren't like that on t' telly.

Where they said it would be a bargain.
Well, was it? Not a lot!
Stuck there in the bedroom,
full of underwear and socks.

Until it collapsed completely,
Well I think the cat attacked it.
Now it's gone the way of most things,
in pieces, in the attic.

When I was a skinny slip of a boy,
Starting at secondary school,
the teachers asked us to choose,
between the woodwork and metalwork rooms.

Well, I was undecided, I didn't relish
the thought of either,
So when they asked me to my face,
I went and said ; 'Me? Neither!'

But I sort of found a reason.
I said ; 'Woodwork, Mr. Higgs.
If I can have some chippings,
for my guinea pigs!'

It was a lesson I grew to hate.
I spent most of my time,
Trying to avoid it,
because I couldn't saw in straight lines.

The saw would go all wobbly and then I'd start to sweat.
I'd see the other boys grinning and how could I forget,
the sarcasm of the master.
'Call that a dovetail joint!' he said.
So, I crawled back into my woodwork
and wished that I was dead.

Well, I made a teapot stand that didn't.
Was it useful? I had my doubts!
Because when you put the teapot on it,
The blooming tea, slopped out!

I made a tea tray, with sloping handles.
One went up and one went down
and you had to be a contortionist
to carry your food around.

You know, even nowadays,
When I use a hammer and nails I sweat.
And I pray no one is looking,
Just in case I get,
my nails half way in,
but sort of curled and bent,
so I have to use my pliers
and once again relent.

Wishing I had not started,
knowing I just can't win.
Waiting for my wife to say,
'I'll get a real man in!'

So, is it any wonder,
when there are jobs to be in,
You'll find me hiding in my little room,
Writing poems like this one!

Some folks get quite excited at a 'DO IT ALL!'
They stride in through the doors full of zest.
But me I'm waiting for a 'DONE IT ALL!'
I think *that* store - will suit me best!

Robert Taylor

That's Life

There are those adverts on T.V.
Showing life as it should be,
people devoted and happy.
Not upset.

Use my brand and you'll live longer,
take this course, I'll make you stronger,
learn to speak in Bonga Bonga.
(four cd's!)

It's the alarm clock telling you
it's a work day once again.
It's a carefully laid out plan
come to a sticky end.
It's an unwelcome visit from some unexpected friends.
That's Life.

It's when the other man's grass seems greener.
His four wheel God seems cleaner.
His wife looks fitter, leaner.
That's life.

It's that letter in the post,
The bill you dread the most.
It's a wet day on the coast.
(with your relations!)

It's being stuck in heavy traffic.
It's building train sets in the attic.
It's a brand new automatic.
(For some!)

It's the time when you are yelling,
That you can't take any more.
When a night out on the tiles,
Is like laying on the floor.
It's when the man from the lottery
is knocking on next door.
That's life!

It's when you hope and pray,
That the garage man will say,
'Your car's passed - take it away!'
That's life.

It's a sudden burst of emotion,
A wife's tender devotion,
when at last, you've got promotion.
(instead of failing again!)

It's that buzzing in your head.
It's making love in bed.
It's playing golf instead!
That's life.

It's a tune that's on your mind.
It's a critic who is unkind.
It's a barmaid yelling time.
That's life.

It's when you're home too late,
and the dog's just had your steak,
and your Van Gogh's just a fake.
(And your Renoir!)

It's the times when you don't win,
when you take it on the chin.
Your horse came in fourth again!
(It might as well be last!)

It's the dentist with his drill,
It's when you forget to take your pill,
It's when you're staggering up that hill.
(with lots of shopping!)

It's when you're stuck in a dreadful jam,
Or your wheel falls off your pram.
Or seven kids are yelling 'MAM !!!
We're so hungry!'

It's when your life's a dull routine.
Or life resembles a battle scene.
It's when the tax inspector's been.
(And your skint again!)

It's when your younger brother's just a pest.
Or your house is a total mess.
Or your son's beaten you at chess.
(And he's only eight!)
It's a spot that's on your tongue.
Or a wart that's on your thumb.
Or a boil down on your bum!
(That's so uncomfortable!)

It's when you're stuck in an exam room with a difficult sort of sum.
Or next door's little brat has a brand new birthday drum!
Or your stuck outside of Woolworth's and you find....
Your date don't ....come.
That's life.

That's Life.

Robert Taylor

A leak in the head

I was at a school in Darlington.
I had just finished a performance
Before about three hundred children
And I left the hall sweating profusely.

I was greeted by a small boy,
Aged about five, who declared;
'Mr! Have you got a leak in your head?'

I wiped the sweat from my brow,
Laughed loudly, and said;
'Mm, Yes. I suppose I must have!'

Robert Taylor

Bath Time!

At another school in Northumberland,
A small child wandered into the hall
as I was packing up at the end of my poetry performance.

He noticed that I was sweating too.
He said, somewhat puzzled ;
'Have you just had a bath?'
I laughed and said;
'Oh yes. I have!'
The child smiled and said;
'I didn't know you were 'lowd to have baths in school!'

Robert Taylor

It didn't work for me!

When your work place is in chaos
and the paper work stacks up by the mile,
you just bite into that chocolate bar
and you'll be far away on a south sea isle.
Where Hawaiian guitars are playing
and girls in tiny grass skirts dance,
and the sound of rippling waves,
will send you in a trance……..

Huh ! I bought *that* bar the other day,
The inside bit was white,
But did it work for me?
No, it was over in three bites.
I'm sure it's a wonderful chocolate bar
because I've seen it on T.V.
where it seemed to work for them,
but it didn't work for me!

When I was quite a bit younger,
I gave the disco scene a whirl,
But being rather shy,
I wasn't too good with girls.
I was one and there were many,
Who wasted half their time,
stuck on the side of the dance floor,
thinking of chat up lines.
Sipping expensive pints,
while wondering who to ask.
The alcohol was there, to make it fun and not a task.

Now one night, a girl smiled straight at me,
It may have been a trick of the light.
But she turned and said to her mate;
' 'Cor! He's a bit of alright!'
Well, I fancied her too. Not half!
So, I thought I'd take my chance.
I had three quick pints for courage
and then I sidled on to dance.
But as she turned, she saw me,
in the savage glare of light.

and gasped ;
'Huh ! You're a spotted Herbert!
Hello and goodnight!'
Well, I crawled home all dejected.
Vowed: 'I'll not go there no more!'

When I saw up on a hoarding,
'Spotty? Try our wonder cure!
Just rub our lotion on your face
and your spots will disappear.
Within a few weeks, your skin will be,
smooth and soft and clear.'

I bought a tube the next day
and followed their instructions to the letter
and every night I looked in the mirror
to see if my spots were better.
I used it for one week,
For two and then for three
and through all my teenage years
but it - didn't work for me!

Then there is that after shave,
Not the cheap and nasty kind.
But the other with a fragrance,
which drives women out of their minds.
It's the one, where when you use it,
You dare not wear a vest.
Because the women rip it off
to caress your hairy chest.
And you have to fight them off.
They chase after you down the street.
But *you* get to pick and choose
the ones you want to meet.
Long legged girls, with pouting lips
and long and milky white thighs.
Flowing, silky hair, with come to bed, sort of eyes.

Well, I bought two bottles of that fluid,
I splashed it on my cheeks and chin,
but all it ever did for them,
was make them ruddy sting!
And did it pull the girls, Oh, No!
So where did I go wrong?
All I ever heard from them was -
'Enid! What's that funny pong?'

I didn't want a queue of girls,
in suspenders and fishnet tights.
The sort with lots of energy,
Who keep you up half the night.
I just wanted an homely lass,
one just like my mum.
Who would bring me cocoa up to bed

And say ; 'How about it chum?'

I tried being generous to a fault
and oozing charm and wit.
I tried getting girls extremely drunk
But that only works a bit.

Oh yes! And I tried all those wonder products
As seen on my T.V.
Where it always worked for them -
But it didn't work for me!

Robert Taylor

Burns Night

I was about to perform my poetry at a school in Edinburgh and the children
were filtering into the hall class by class.
I was intrigued to hear one of the male members of staff laughing as his class
filed in. When I asked him what he was laughing at he told me that he had
overheard this conversation on his way into the hall -

BOY 1: What are we going to see?

BOY 2: Oh, some poet or other!

BOY 1: Oh, what's his name?

BOY 2: It's Robert somebody or other.

BOY 1: Robert? Robert? Oh, I know who it'll be. It'll be that - Robert Burns!

Please Note -   I do hope that they weren't too disappointed at getting me
instead of "Scotland's most famous poet!"

Robert Taylor

The dog walker's lament.

Outside the rain is pouring
And I hear they forecast snow.
The sharp north wind is howling
And when you've got to go, you go.

This hound he has no hatred,
for wind or rain or snow.
He only knows its 'walkies' time.
And when he goes......I go!

He lifts a demanding paw
and boffs me on the knee.
His large brown eyes adore me,
Show that he's fond of me.

Besides, he knows that it's time,
For me foul weather coat again.
My wellies, my scarf and gloves
and to trudge out into the rain.

This dog has little patience,
he doesn't like to wait.
He puts his paws up on my shoulders
and tells me to my face.

And if you should pass our house
Any time after nine,
You might see this streaky brown thing,
dragging me behind.

He knows when it's time to drag me,
passed lamp posts, bushes and trees
which he can cock his leg against
and do his Q's and P's!

And then he'll haul me home again,
shivering and soaked to the skin.
But he'll insist on a bit of sniffing first,
where other dogs have been.
Then when we're back in the house
and I'm free from my protective gear,
he'll stand in the middle of the kitchen
and shake himself everywhere!
He has hidden hordes of strength
and he's such an awkward critter
And he's never heard of manners

but I think he's made me fitter.

My wife got him for her twenty first -
a large dog with a long pedigree.
Her father paid the seventy quid,
but who gets to do the walking - ME!

On our wedding day I remember,
Her father gave the two of them away.
My wife and her dog –
two licences to pay.

Her father, in his reception speech,
(which he enjoyed I could tell!)
He said, 'I'm not only losing a daughter
but a large mad dog as well!'

Outside the rain is pouring
and it's turning into snow.
And the sharp north wind is howling,
But now I've got to go -   I'll go!

Robert Taylor

A Great Poemer!

After one particular performance at a school, somewhere in Yorkshire.
I was greeted by a young girl who beamed
Form ear to ear, as she declared;
'You're a *great poemer* you!'

I was pleased to be a *'great poemer!'*

P.S. I got to thinking afterwards.
        Perhaps you could have – ' great poemists!' too!

P.S.S. I'd love to be one of those too. But I'm not greedy!

Robert Taylor

A special day out

'*Flamin Azaleas!*'
It sounded like swearing
But it was an apt description
Of what we were seeing,
'*Oooh its googy the colour of a monkeys doodah*
She giggles, knowing she's been unable to find
The words she wanted
We walked on, knowing nonsense.
She chattering nothings,
But squeezing my arm and smiling and smiling.
I wondered at the brain slowly slipping,
Each day more nibbled
Each zapping away
What we have shared.
I grow weary,
Lunch beckons.
Oh good, the menu has pictures
She stabs at them with firm finger
'*That's it, that's the one, Lassieagna!*'
'It's lasagne Mum, you don't like it.'
She folds her arms
A sulky child
'*Do,do like it!*'
I sigh and order.
In my heart
Disorder,
Dismay,
Disarray.
The plate is placed with a smile
She pushes it away,
Violence, a never before companion
Erupts,
'*What the hell did you get me that for?*
Foreign muck
If that's me dinner when's me tea?'
I look at her through tears
Thin summer dress, loose flapping
Bones protruding
There's always a reason not to eat,
She always needs reminding…
Of everything.

Joyce Worsfold

113

George – A Melodrama.

In city streets –
Highways, byways and buildings;
George.
In bus shelters; waiting.
In pub forecourts; drinking.
So small,
under the sun,
where nothing is new.
An inferior, insignificant, tiny George.

George -
With one pound coin firm in hand.
One pound of purchasing power!
Bus stop. Bus.
'A red one!' He snarls. 'I'll pay in cash.'
And soon the city.

City lights, buildings, dozens of buildings.
Excitement.
A whole new world!
George transfixed. Overcome with emotion.
As metre after metre of universe
is revealed, before his very eyes.
Taking it all in, every detail,
must not miss one single detail.
All this for a soft, textured red one,
which tears easily in the hand.
What power!

George.
Home again.
Happy days.
A spider on the bathroom wall.
Wife in towel. Screams!
And there is George.
Our hero.
The Times colour supplement - a first time hit!
One dead spider.
One impressed wife.
More power.

George.
Wage earner.
Protector of wife,
in this huge, cruel, selfish world.

Proud and tall against spiders
and bus tickets which tear easily!

Executioner of numerous spiders!
Accumulator of one pound coins!
A bold, superior, so tall, George.

Though, many suns later,
Separate beds.
The smell of sex confused with early coffee.
Occasionally forced smiles between cornflake boxes,
morning post
and newspapers.

George.
Stout bellied,
Small and fat,
against the sun.
Bedroom just another room.
All secrets gone.
But - bread winner.
Reaping benefits of many years before the office desk.
Season ticket at united.
Golf club subscriptions fully paid up.
Small, but compact caravan, by the coast.

Successful – but numb.
Powerful – but paranoid.
(too many spiders buildings cobwebs, no longer impressed wife).
One pound coins – far too frequent now.
No purchasing power.
Buses, cities, lights, buildings ; All the same.
No fun.
Spider stamping all behind him now.
(Now a red letter day- means, final fuel bill!)

But George,
Philosophical as ever, contemplates;
"When the lights go out, you soon find out who your friends are."

And now the lights are going out all over the city.
And George, is wondering,
Just how dark –
it can get.

Robert Taylor

Silent Night

Phone rings, Heart sinks
Cover ears, Quell my fears
Pick it up, Look at clock
Midnight strikes, Mum speaks,
'They're driving me mad
They're singing again
They've been at it all day,
They'll be sorry!
I've called the police
AND environmental health!
They'll be sorry
They didn't invite me!
Listen! Can you hear them?'
Silence
'Well?'
'I can't hear them mother'
Phone goes dead.

I pick up my car-keys
And drive through the dark,
oil-black lanes
Eerie motorways.
As I drive down her street,
A police-car is just leaving
Two laughing policemen
Joking about a madwoman
In the flat they've just left.
I hang back
And when they've gone,
Quietly let myself in.
Mum's standing at the top of the stairs
Angry and weeping.
I take her hand
And lead her like a little child
'Listen!' she says
They're doing it again, singing'
Head on one side she conducts
And joins the imaginary refrain,
'How great thou art
How great thou art'
It's her favourite hymn
But only she hears it
In the silence of the night.'

Joyce Worsfold

Funeral Teas

Three p.m.
Better ring Mum again.
No answer
Stress seethes snake-like
Through stomach and chest
Head throbs, I pace
I scrub, I pace
I try again.
She answers on the tenth ring,
'Mum, where were you?'
'The ambulance has just left'.
'What ambulance?'
'The one I rang for, for May,
They were too late
She's passed on
Dead and gone!
I watched through the window
It just came and went again.'

'Mum, it's O.K. our Sue will be there soon'
'I knew it would happen when I saw the moon!'
'Mum, I love you!'
'What will I do without my best friend?
I'm sick of all this, will it ever end?
The phone goes dead.
Oh, my throbbing head.
Then it shrills again.
' Hello love, I'm worried about your Mum
Do you think that you can come,
You'll never guess what she's just done!'

Eight p.m.
My sister rings and sobs her tale.
'When I got in you should have seen the spread
She had all the leaves of the table out
The embroidered cloth with the crinoline ladies
Napkins folded like water-lilies
Beautifully cut sandwiches, brown and white bread
Neat triangles on plates with labels that said
Salmon, corned beef and potted meat
Eggs and tuna and cheese with beet.
There were shop bought cakes ranged in dishes
She had waited and waited for them all to come
For May's funeral tea that should have started at one!

Joyce Worsfold

A Widow's Tale. (I miss him!)

I can't get used to him not being here.
Not surprising that - when we shared everything for over fifty years.
We met in out teens. It seems like yesterday in some ways.
And now? What keeps me going I don't know.
I miss him.

The day before he died we found this video in a charity shop.
It was a film we had seen - oh, years ago. In our teens.
He said; 'Look Jean! Do you remember this?'
I said; 'Remember it? I remember where and when we first saw it!'
And we both said together; 'The Tivoli. 1951.'
He said; 'yes, it was our third date.'
And I said, 'No, it was the fourth.'
And he said ; 'Well, only you count the night I went down to your house and we
walked to the fish shop together. I didn't call that a date.'
Well, I did.
We bought the video. It was only a pound. We watched it and laughed, until the
tears came down our cheeks.
'Great film that!' He said. 'I think we'll go back next week and get another. You
can't beat it at that price.'
That night, I laid awake for half an hour listening to him snoring. Len used to
snore like the bombs in the blitz. Every so often, it sounded more like an
extrocet missile. Not that I've heard one - but I've heard they are noisy and Len's
snoring was certainly that!
I woke him as usual with great difficulty - I tried first, using my bony elbows and
I dug him in the ribs; I tried shaking him, words in the ear and finally a yell - and
that did the trick.
He looked at me, slightly confused, and said-
'Huh! Huh! Was I snoring again?'
'Yes, Len.' I said. 'We've had complaints from The Whitakers.'
'The Whitakers?' He said. 'Don't be daft. They live three streets away!'
'Exactly!' I said triumphantly. 'Which shows you how loud your snoring is!'
'Right,' He said smiling. 'I'll go in the spare room.'
'Good.' I said. 'I might get some sleep now.'

The next morning, I found him in there - dead.
A massive heart attack apparently. It had been coming for a while, but it was still
a great shock. I really felt guilty about it.
If only he had stayed with me in bed, I might have realised what was happening
and been able to call the ambulance and saved him. If I had not sent him into
that spare room he might still be here.
The experts tell me otherwise, but we'll never know for sure.

Hee, I'd give anything to hear him snoring again, next to me in bed. Now.
I'd say, 'Snore as much as you want Len. It's better than you not being here!'
I miss him.

I miss him, when there is a joke on the T.V. or radio or in a magazine. Something we can laugh about together. Somehow, jokes don't seem as funny when there is no one there to share them with.

I can still see him now, sitting here at the dining room table, making his plastic model planes or ships as he was apt to do. There would be a bit of aeroplane in one hand....a tube of glue in the other....and his glasses perched on the end of his nose,
chuntering away to himself, about which part goes where.

Sometimes, I go into a room and out of it again. I return to the room after a deep breath, hoping I've got it wrong. Hoping that the next time I return, Len will there with his models and glue and his glasses and his chuntering........

I sometimes, set two places for dinner. I buy two pieces of meat or fish - instead of the one. I make tea for two.

And say; 'Flippin' heck! I'll have to drink them both now. You can't go wasting tea! But I nearly always end up throwing one of them away after its gone cold.

I catch myself saying; 'You can't drink out of that cup. That's Len's cup.'
Two hours later, I'll throw away the tea - cold.

And I'll say to Len's photo on the mantelpiece. 'Len! You've done it again lad! You've let your tea go cold! Please come back and drink it!'

If folks could hear me, they'd say, 'Silly old bat!
Poor old bird's going soft in the head!'

And time drifts by and I suddenly find myself hours later.....sitting in the darkness. I look at the clock and say; 'Blimey! It's nine o clock! I've gone and missed Coronation Street again!'

Ironic really, when we have so little time left, we end up wasting a lot of it!

It's a good job I've got a cat and budgie for company. They are my best friends now. They are both good listeners - that's what I love about them - better than Len used to be, to be honest. They don't interrupt either that's what I like about them. I spend hours telling them about what Len and I used to get up to. About all the places we've been to and the people we've met. Occasionally the cat will get up and leave as if to say; 'I've heard enough of this story now.......I'm off!'

Then the budgie, (stuck in his cage, so he can't leave), sometimes turns his back on me now and again and starts chirping. As though to say -
'I've had enough of that story too.'

A while before Len died, I drew some money out of the building society for a short trip we were planning. It was £300 - which was quite a lot of money to us.

I was walking down the street in town, when a young couple approached and she very charmingly asked for directions.

I turned to point down the street, when the young man grabbed my handbag, with the £300 inside and ran off down the street.

I was mortified.

When I got home I thought that Len might be angry with me, but he was not. He gave me a cuddle. And said what he often said;
'Never mind lass. It's not that important. In the scheme of things, it's just a little thing. A little mishap. Not that important at all.'

And when I cried with anger about the wickedness of people and how unfair life could be ....
He said; 'Look, don't worry. I'm here. It's you and me against the world dear. You and me. And we'll pull through. We will. We'll pull through.'

Except it's not him and me against the world any more - is it! It's just me! So, I'll guess I shall just have to pull through on my own.
I miss him though.

I've got bingo tonight. With Rose and Mary. They're widows too. We've that that much in common. It will be bingo, followed by fish and chips and a DVD at Mary's place. It's turning into a right little weekly do. We have a laugh and it takes our minds off things for a while.
Until I get home and stare at Len's photo on the mantelpiece and say;
'We had a laugh tonight Len. But it was not like you and me. Not the same. Never will be.'
Then I give his photo a wee kiss and try not to feel sad. Len might have gone - but not the memories. They will always remain.
Then the budgie chirps and the cat purrs and I sup hot tea and I – 'Keep on, keeping on!' (I heard that in song today!)

I shall *'Keep on! Keeping on!'*
What *else* can I do?

Robert Taylor

My Mum.

My mum has Alzheimer's.
She does not recognise her family anymore.
She stares passed you into some far off distant place,
where she can still go.
When she's there, she visits some of the people and some of the things she knew -
Long, long ago.

A fair while ago,
When I visited her, after sadly, not doing so for some time,
due to the many miles between us,
she suddenly looked at me with a spark of recognition
and said, to the surprise of both my sisters.

'You know who you remind me of?'

And I said. 'I don't know, who?'

'You look a bit like our Robert!' she said smiling.

'That's because I am your Robert!' I replied, smiling back eagerly.

She looked back at me with some disbelief – tinged almost with disgust.
'Don't be *silly,*' She said. 'No! You're *not him!* You can't be him!
You don't even *look* like him!'

I wanted to argue, and tell her that I *was* indeed *him.*
Her son!   Robert!
But then I realised that there was no point in arguing.
To her, I was not her son.
She has not got a son anymore.
She has no daughters either.

She has no family left at all.

Except for her adopted family -
The nurses and carers who look after her on a daily basis –
and have done for years.
Everyone else –
are just *visitors.*
Strange, occasional, visitors.

Robert Taylor

All things, daffodils

It's a long drive
And I always worry
What I'll find
When I arrive.

She sits unseeing
'Hello Mum!'
'I'm not'
'Not What?'
'Not Mum
I'm nobody's Mum
My name is Violet'
*'Hello Violet
My name is Joyce'*
'Pleased to meet you'
Oh Mum!
*'Would you like to come
For a cup of tea?'*
'Bugger off'
'Come on, let's put the kettle on'
'I'm too busy
I've got a lot to do.
Go ask someone else
I don't want to talk to you.'
'Look I've brought you daffodils!'
Edna, in the next chair
Comes out of her frozen stare
Leaps to her feet her shoulders back
And says
'Daffodils', by William Wordsworth
I wondered lonely as a cloud
That floats on high o'er vales and hills
And all at once I saw a crowd, a host, of golden daffodils'
She continues to recite
Each word clearly enunciated
Eyes alive and bright
Her being concentrated.
Suddenly Mum
Not to be outdone
Stands up beside her,
And begins her recitation
'All things bright and beautiful
All creatures great and small.
All things wise and wonderful
The Lord God made them all.'

We all marvelled at these perfect renditions
So hard to understand this most destroying of conditions.
We clapped loudly and cheered
This was not what I had feared.
They did a stately minuet
And curtsied proud
And I praised the Lord,
For these sweet memories found.

Joyce Worsfold

Remembering Rock and Roll

Singer unwinds wire from microphone
Fiddles and faffs; testing testing 1,2,3.
Audience move restlessly.
Rosie sits all alone
Rosie rocks with face of stone
Dora drags daisy by the hand
They walk incessantly, round and round.
Barbara perambulates, wringing her hands
Staring, sieved mind longing to understand.
Rosie sits all alone
Rosie rocks with face of stone.
Audrey groans an endless monotone
Gordon grins
The singer sings.
Carers cajole
Touch shoulders
Hug and hold
The singer talks.
It leaves them cold.
Rosie sits all alone
Rosie rocks with face of stone.
The singer tries, looking weary
'It's a long way to Tipperary'
Blank faces reflect back.
'Pack up your troubles in your old kit bag'
Sorry, not possible, so much gone
Erased by the rubber of age
Important print an empty page.
People, places things to fear
Call, then fade and disappear.
Rosie sits all alone
Rosie rocks with face of stone.
The singer tries another beat, Rhythms rock
There is a tap of slippered feet.
Rock around the clock
Dora and Daisy come alive
Stop shuffling and start to jive
Barbara smiles a hazy recognition
But Rosie undergoes a startling transformation,
Eyes alight and such a smile, radiates glory, good and grace.
A carer gasps at the luminous beauty of her face,
Tears fall
Laughter leaps
Rosie smiles... *and we all weep.*

Joyce Worsfold

Down the Line

There's nothing I like better,
When he's out at his golf club,
Than to curl up in an easy chair,
with my CD's and a book.

I sit listening to Chopin carried on the wing.
I listen to those octaves,
I hear that piano sing.

I dreamt once of being a pianist,
I had lessons at x pounds a time,
but the exercises seemed dull
and I never practiced.
It's one thing I regret - down the line.

I can play a bit, hymns at Christmas,
Tipperary, that kind of thing,
I can play Fur Elise and The Entertainer,
But then who can't? They're not everything.

I sometimes imagine myself as Liszt - female,
thundering up and down those keys.
Or playing some heartfelt melody,
That reminds one, of a gentle summer breeze.
Chopin gets to me, as much as anyone -
I love Schubert, Schumann, Liszt - and also - Rachmaninoff.
They don't have soul, these modern composers.
They are somehow lacking for me.
I'd like to have been a pianist,
starring with the L.S.O.
When the conductor raised his baton
I'd flex my fingers, all ready to go.

Funny thing the passing of time,
Once gone it's *never* retrievable.
It's one thing I regret down the line.
But *I listen* as much as I'm able.

Robert Taylor

The Photograph.

I found this photograph today in a cupboard I haven't cleared out for years.
Shame on me! I'm such a slut! There was the photo and a letter.
They were from Andrew -
my first proper boyfriend all those years ago.
He looked like George Harrison of the Beatles.
He even had the Beatles mop hair cut.
And everyone who saw him, did a double take.
'Is it really him? No, it can't be. He wouldn't here in Leeds sat in a pub with a
girl. No! He would be away on tour with the Beatles- somewhere exotic!'
Andrew - because that was his real name, used to love it of course, and when he
was asked for an autograph, he signed it 'All my love from George H.'
He loved that too. Mind you, anyone who ever heard him try to sing, would
have soon known that he was not the real thing! He had an atrocious singing
voice! He couldn't play guitar either. He tried but couldn't. His plectrum spent
more time in the hole in the middle of his guitar – than gently caressing the
strings.
He was good looking though. And though I am loath to admit it, looking like one
of the Beatles, not only gave *him* some sort celebrity status- It gave *me* status too!
It made other girls envious of me!
'Fancy going out with someone who looks like a Beatle! You lucky thing!'
They'd tell me.
I felt lucky too. Mind you, that did have a down side. Other girls were always
chasing him. Some would even do it blatantly - right there in front of me - others,
like some of my - so called best friends - would do it behind my back.
Andrew and I, only lasted a few months together. Though he was the best
looking fellow I ever dated and probably the funniest, he was not the one for me.
He had a long line of girlfriends afterwards - even a few on the side, whilst he
was going out with *me* no doubt! I did hear lots of rumours.
But I was his first girlfriend - and he was my first boyfriend! They can't take that
away from me!
When George Harrison died, from cancer, tragically young, in his fifties, I cried
for days. I felt that, I was not only losing a Beatle, (a group I had worshipped!)
but a vital part of my past life. I hope, that makes some sort of sense.
One day, I got on the bus to town and the driver stared at me and said hello.
He was fat, balding and middle aged.
'Don't you recognise me?' He asked. 'You went out with my older brother -
Andrew. Don't you remember?'
'James!' I said. 'Gosh! How is Andrew?'
'He's okay.' he said. 'He's just got married again for the fourth time.'
'Fourth time!' I said.
'Yes.' He said, laughing. 'He can't seem to keep a wife. He lives in Devon now
though. He's a pig farmer.'
'Is he?' I said, laughing. 'Has he still got the George Harrison good looks?'
'No! Goodness gracious, no! You must be joking.' He said. 'He's actually, got
less hair than I have now! And he's fatter than me!'
I looked at his large paunch hanging over the wheel, smiled, paid my fare and

sat down.

I closed my eyes and saw an apparition. A slim, delicate, fairly trendy blonde, walking hand in hand on the beach with a slim, mop haired, good looking, young man - who looked awfully like George Harrison of the Beatles.
The image lasted, just as long as I kept my eyes tightly closed.

When the bus hit a bump and I lurched forward in my seat and opened my eyes, the image had gone.
I tried – but I could not get it back.
Tut! Tut! Best leave it where it is I suppose- something from my far distant past.
But why, does it - in some ways – feel like it was only - *yesterday?*

Robert Taylor

Breakdown

Fat fingers first began to model delusion.
warm in summer darkness beneath sheets
smelling of persil and the west wind,
Her mind rolled and stretched,
Sandwiched between waking and sleeping
she savoured it's softness.
She would be Doris Day with a secret love,
Judy Garland, a seductive Monroe
each illusion she coiled and curved to the shape
of her own design and entered a place of tall trees and damp earth,
nightingales and damask light.
Later, she pinched and shaped to precise specifications,
A man suave, dark
Impressive house, classic car
odourless babies
clothes from Marks and Spencers,
holidays in Spain.
All occurred in strict rotation.

The wheel spun faster,
spurting clay slipping through fingers.
out of control
and all around
shapeless lumps, broken pots.
She entered a place of mud
where roots slaked entrails
and crows clawed.

She sits on mottled grass
rolling blu-tak between thumb and finger,
waiting for the trees and birds to mend.

Joyce Worsfold

128

Going Out

Barbara's on a mission,
the door, the door.
Cannot be deflected
By the door, the door.
Doors used to open
People have gone out.
There is an out.
She's seen it
Through the window.
But the door doesn't open for Barbara.
The door is a barrier to life.
So many troubles to untangle
So much string to unwind.

The filing system is jumbled
Some of the files have gone.
And Barbara is constantly grasping,
Reaching out and remembering all wrong.
Once she pigeonholed important papers.
The public depended on her.
Her efficiency was really daunting,
Organization was her second nature.
But now, everything is awry,
Out of kilter, misaligned, skew wiff
And it can't be helped by an appraisal
Or stiff drink, or a smoke or a spliff.

She's a wafer of her former self.
She finds it difficult to eat.
Her carefully prepared, nutritious lunch
lies untouched,
though she likes the occasional sweet.
She never responds to questions,
They're too painful to unravel.
But compliments she understands
They're not meaningless gabble.
"Your hair looks nice today, Barbara."
Elicits a smile.
"That colour suits you."
Brings a beam that transforms for a while,
"But where is your slipper?"
As she lopsidedly lurches about,
brings not a glimmer or grasp.
She just stares into the distance
where once more sensible questions were asked.
She stumbles from door to the window

For days she uttered not a word.
When suddenly an animated observance
Miraculously is heard.
"There's a rabbit out in the garden,
It's jumping about.
I like to see rabbits – the brown ones.
when I go out!'

Joyce Worsfold

Our Joannie.

Our Joannie used to come and see us.
She came at least twice every week.
But now she hardly ever comes near us.
She doesn't write, or phone, we hardly speak.
She always brought a smile to his face
in a way that I never could.
She was the brightest thing in our lives,
What made her change I never understood.
We gave her everything that we could,
We built our lives round our little girl.
Dolls houses, parties and pantomimes,
She was the best thing in our world.
This photo is on the beach at Brighton.
('Yes, I remember!')
This one a day trip to Ostend.
('I can't forget that!')
This one was taken in Majorca.
('Oh, was it?')
And this one was with her first boyfriend.
('Oh, *him! Never liked him!'*)
One should never look back.
One should always look ahead. Start anew.
But when you get to our age,
That's not easy to do.
We gave so much to our Joannie,
but one thing makes me mad,
amongst the things we gave her,
were all the faults we had!

It's a shame she is so unhappy,
She could make someone a good wife.
But it doesn't matter what we tell her,
Each must live their own life.
(We give and take. We make mistakes).
We haven't got that much one common,
Alf and I.
We're like the old folks on the hill,
Derby and Joan, without their Joannie.
Waiting for - the Winter's chill.

Oh. Joannie! *Please* give us back - *our* lives!

Robert Taylor

Michael

Michael was a friend.
At least, we worked together.
Exchanged pleasantries, about current affairs,
football and the weather.
We shared clues for "The mirror" crossword,
Over tea and toast each tea break.

Michael hung himself the other day.
He bought some rope. He made a noose.
He closed the curtains, so no one could see.
Then hung himself from the ceiling.
He was 22. A policeman cut him down.

Michael was quiet in manners and speech.
Nervous, inoffensive and sensitive;
Maddeningly slow, but meticulous at work.
Why did he choose to die?
I cannot pretend to know.
If there were signs, I never saw them.
I cannot pretend I saw them.

But he took some rope. He made a noose.
He closed the curtains so no one could see.
Then hung himself from the ceiling.
He was 22. And he chose to die.

He had been away for three days.
I missed him for the two.
Perhaps he'd caught a cold I thought,
or a touch of flu.

Yesterday, the manager broke the news.
All day it was a talking point.
Well, that and the team for Saturday's match with Liverpool.
He was 22. A policeman cut him down.

Today, I check orders, count stock and balance books.
Tomorrow, they bury Michael.
I have written this, just to record his death.

Robert Taylor

Finale

A neighbour arrives with her paraphernalia
cradles carnations oasis, ribbon
"Just give me a corner and I'll get cracking"
Arthritic fingers circle stems
Coax, press, position,
"Aye it's slow work but I'd like to do it"
Wicker basket, maiden fern, fat pinks
scent of cinammon and damp grass.

A woman with a zimmer and a walnut face
brings a bunch of sweet peas.
You bury your face in them, scent intensified by tears,
I avert my eyes to a lustre jug filled with golden Whiskey Mac
winking on the mantle flanked by cards.

A formality of aunts, crammed in the kitchen
chopping and gratingand assembling quiches.
Two sponges from a cousin in Berkshire
sandwiched with cream from her own cows.

I polish the Waterford bowl
and watch it filled
kiwi fruit and nectarines
peaches and tangerines
'The strawberries were half price at Sainsbury's'
'No...we'll leave the banana till last
  No point in taking chances"
"No paper plates, she wouldn't have liked it
Lucy next door is bringing her Wedgewood
Jean over the road her Royal Albert
and of course there's our Lady Carlyle.
Don't forget to polish the legs of the table."
I lay the crystal glass in serried rows
and watch the laser show
as they catch the sun.
I pour sherry and smile.
You want no wreaths
no weeping in corners.
We put her to rest
with roses and Rachmaninov
and with Vivaldi by Nigel Kennedy
because she thought him such a clever lad.
She always said, "Have your cake whilst you've still got your teeth."

Joyce Worsfold

Death in the high street.

I stood outside the bank when the payroll was due.
Smiled when I saw the popgun and masks
and looked for the camera crew.
A weedy man, with spectacles crumpled and fell.
No Oscar winning fall,
just a pathetic plunge.
And the blood was most un-ketchup like.
And the cries of the extras seemed melodramatic.
When the bad men drove off in a car, in a hurry,
I still did not understand it fully.
I stayed frozen to the spot,
While the weedy man died, before my eyes.
Call me a coward, call me shocked,
But I stood unbelieving, while the weedy man died.

I've seen it in the papers now.
(Alas! Someone had a camera!)
And I still can't believe it was real.
There's a picture of the man as he died,
And behind him in the picture stands a man who – *smiled.*

Robert Taylor

Afterwards

Almost silence
Clock ticks
You read
My chubby infant hands grasp
His green-marbled fountain pen
Pages of flowing script
Are scattered on red chenille cloth
Lifeless bodies on a bloody sea
No recognisable words,
Copper-plate nonsense drips
From the pen
That once said so much more.
The coals drop in the fire's blaze
Kettle hisses on the hob of the blackened range
I sit beside the glow
Back toasted by the oven door,
Important missives forgotten.
You gaze unseeing
Finger the silver wings
Of his airforce, precious things.
In simple silence
You and I sit
There are no words for loss.

Joyce Worsfold

We are but dust

Large or small, walk or crawl,
rise and fall.
All have their time.

Bird or beast, starve or feast,
in west or east.
All have their poem.

Rough or smooth, lies or truth,
age and youth.
All have their song to sing.

Think of the world, turning in space,
Think of the future, of the whole human race,
We are so blessed, and yet we're so cursed.
We are but dust, in the great universe.

Man or boy, gun or toy,
Hate or joy,
All have their day.

Cap or clown, judge or clown,
Up and down,
All have their poem, to rhyme.

We laugh and cry, when and why,
shrug and sigh.
All play their part.

Think of us all, and what we've become,
all going forward, but in different directions.
We are so blessed, and yet we're so cursed,
We are but dust, in the great universe.

Robert Taylor with Mike Hone